John the Baptist in Congress

John the Baptist in Congress

How Christian Philosophy Corrupts
American Government

Jim Duncan

Writer's Showcase
San Jose New York Lincoln Shanghai

John the Baptist in Congress
How Christian Philosophy Corrupts American Government

Writer's Showcase
an imprint of iUniverse, Inc.

For information address:
iUniverse, Inc.
5220 S. 16th St., Suite 200
Lincoln, NE 68512
www.iuniverse.com

ISBN: 0-595-22048-7

Printed in the United States of America

The author gratefully acknowledges permission to quote from the following sources.

Ayn Rand, from **The Virtue of Selfishness**, Copyright 1964 by The Objectivist Newletter Inc., Reprinted by permission of Penguin Putnam Inc.

Edith Hamilton, from **Mythology**, Copyright 1942 by Edith Hamilton. Reprinted by permission of Little, Brown and Company.

Will Durant, from **The Age of Reformation**, Copyright 1957, ISBN: 0-671-61050-5, Reprinted by permission of Simon & Schuster.

Thomas Merton, from **Zen and the Birds of Appetite**, copyright 1968 by The Abbey of Gethsemani Inc., Reprinted by permission of New Directions Publishing Corp.

Ayn Rand, from **The Voice of Reason**, copyright 1990 by Penguin Books. Reprinted by permission of Penguin Putnam Inc.

Eugene Kamenka, translator, from **The Portable Karl Marx**, Copyright 1983 by Viking Penguin Inc., Reprinted by permission of Penguin Putnam Inc.

Contents

Foreword xi

Part I

What is Religion? 3
- *Chronology* *3*
- *Western Religions* *5*
- *Swords and Temples* *6*
- *Anti-mind & Anti-man* *9*
- *Silent* *13*
- *Divisive* *15*
- *Big Business* *16*
- *Religion or Cult* *17*
- *The Fish and the Formula* *19*
- *Credit* *22*

Part II

Reason vs. Non-reason 27
- *Accepting the Absurd* *27*
- *Pick and Choose* *32*
- *Locked In* *34*
- *Cognition or Mysticism* *35*
- *Acquiring and Validating Knowledge* *35*
- *Who Thinks?* *37*

- *Logic and Mysteries* *38*
- *The Bible's Author.* *41*
- *Evaluating Scripture* *42*

Part III

Adventures and Fairy Tales 45

Part IV

According to Luke 65
- *Evil and Anarchy* *65*

Part V

Philosophy for Chaos 83
- *Non-judgment.* *83*
- *Forgiveness* *86*
- *Altruism* *90*

Part VI

The Altruist Ideal 99
- *Good Intentions* *99*
- *Means and Ends* *105*
- *Politics* *109*
- *The Economic Unit.* *110*
- *Basic Instruction on How to be Poor.* *113*
- *Altruism vs. Morality.* *119*

Part VII

The Law and Happiness 127
- *Bruiser* *127*
- *Values.* *132*

- *Don't Kill* *133*
- *Don't Steal* *134*
- *Honesty* *135*
- *Don't Commit Adultery* *136*
- *Happiness and the Rules* *141*
- *About the Outlaws* *142*
- *This Is It* *143*

Epilogue *145*
Bibliography *151*

Foreword

Religions present their followers with a particular view of existence, and that view then becomes an integral part of the basis for their philosophy of life. The ideals of any particular religion thus form the basis for interpersonal relationships and for the political views and laws that are adopted and practiced by its members. Whether its members are devout, casual or skeptical, most accept what they believe to be a fundamental goodness in the philosophy of the religion. The result is that they accept the social philosophy of the religion regardless of their degree of belief in the fundamental teachings of it. In the case of Christians, a person might seriously question the existence of a god, but would accept such concepts as forgiveness and self-sacrifice as a right way of life. They would also expect others to live by similar guidelines. So the philosophy of the religion can dominate a society even though many of its followers doubt the basis of the religion itself.

A book written with the intent to destroy the myth of the Bible would have a very unoriginal and essentially meaningless purpose. After all it should make little difference to one if his neighbor chooses to waste a good portion of his life and money on religious activities. That is certainly his personal choice. But when the philosophy of his religion spills over into the public arena, as it naturally must do, and impacts society in a negative way, it does make a difference.

In 1787, Thomas Jefferson wrote, "Question with boldness even the existence of a god." (1) Nearly two centuries later, Ayn Rand wrote, "America's inner contradiction was the altruist-collectivist ethics. Altruism is incompatible with freedom, with capitalism and with individual rights. One cannot combine the pursuit of happiness with the moral status of a sacrificial animal."(2) The intent of this book is to challenge the philosophy of Christianity, and not just to challenge Biblical myths and the existence of a god. The latter however is necessary in order to attempt to have a clean mental slate to work with. It's necessary to expose the myth of God because it is the basis for the myth of his alleged son and his socialist apostles.

Biblical teachings laid the groundwork for the modern welfare state. From the idea of offerings to God in the Old Testament to collectivism in the New Testament, western civilization has been steeped in the concept of self-sacrifice as a moral virtue. Karl Marx and other advocates of socialism found fertile soil in Christian minds for the evil seeds of their anti-man social philosophies to germinate and prosper in. The welfare state in America expands daily because most Americans believe that the government, i.e., the taxpayers, has a moral obligation to sustain the lives of those who don't do so for themselves. Simultaneously they are angered that their own families are overburdened with the taxes required to support the very programs that they see as virtuous. This contradiction is the direct result of the teachings of John the Baptist and the apostles of Jesus.

John the Baptist was the first to articulate self-sacrifice as a superior virtue in the New Testament. The concept of altruism reached its full potential of collectivism in the book of *The Acts of the Apostles* in the New Testament. Chapter 5, verses 1 through 10 of *Acts*, strongly suggests that their god endorsed collectivism. Karl Marx used the identical concept of the apostles in stating the goal of the welfare state. Since there is no moral/ethical basis for altruism, most of the Christian world was and remains confused about the inverted morality of the apostles and Marx. It is because the Christian mind has been permeated with self-sacrifice as a moral ideal for nearly two thousand years that collectivism is viewed as morally superior to individualism.

This inverted morality instructs us that the needs of the non-producers are morally superior to the needs and wants of the producers. It does not tell us why it is so because it cannot do so, and it never has done so. The American government followed the lead of European governments when it introduced a limited form of the welfare state.

That limited welfare state has since grown into "the great society" in which the property of the producers is routinely confiscated in order to fund the "entitlements" of the needy. Marx would indeed be pleased if he was alive to witness the posthumous success of his political philosophy.

The Biblical view of man as being continually and incorrigibly evil is quite simply false. The New Testament doctrines of non-judgment, forgiveness and altruism are anti-man, and they are destructive to the society that man requires in order for him to survive and to be happy. These might appear to be brash statements. They certainly contradict the view held by many that although God and Jesus as his Son might be myths; the Bible nonetheless provides a viable framework for a healthy society. We will see that only a miniscule part of the Bible provides such a framework. We will see that the core teachings of Jesus and his apostles actually negate the viable aspects of the Bible and tend to corrupt personal and group relationships.

I suggest to you that man is indeed selfish. Everything in his genetic makeup drives him continually to seek his survival, safety and personal gratification. This is not the same as to say that his every thought is evil. Selfishness is not evil. I also suggest that it is mans right, even his moral duty, to seek his personal happiness, and that a rational man can continually do so and be a good member of his society at the same time. There is no contradiction between being selfish and being a good neighbor and a good citizen. Being selfish is natural. Being a good neighbor and a good citizen is being rational. A rational man can be totally selfish and a model neighbor and citizen.

The process of debunking the Bible and the corrupt philosophy of Christianity, particularly altruism, has four essential parts. The nature of religion, its origin and its impact on man must be examined. Man's ability to validate his reason in the face of the critics of reason and the faithful must be established, and then the critique of scripture can begin. The chaos producing teachings of non-judgment, forgiveness and altruism can then be challenged. This book accomplishes those assignments in parts I through VI. Part VII validates the need for rules within society and some of the laws of Moses because they are necessary for man in his search for happiness. The currently popular and inverted moral view that the financially successful have some kind of debt to society that must be "paid back" is addressed in the epilogue. There we will see that society is in debt to the entrepreneurs, and that the full indebtedness can never be repaid.

This is a small book to stand up to and criticize the very voluminous Bible. Although the Bible is very large, it is fundamentally simple, and its philosophical teachings are few. It would take several volumes to dispel every myth in it. That isn't necessary. It is sufficient to discredit enough of its fundamentals to establish the fact that most of it is impossible, and that none of it is probable. That is accomplished in this book. I believe that if the Bible were to be published today for the very first time that most readers would discard it as the work of a lunatic before they completed reading Genesis. Any reader with even a basic understanding of astronomy, natural science and logic would evaluate it as trash. Those who took the trouble to read all of it would demand that it should be "X" rated.

The book is not intended to be entertaining nor simply informative. It is intended to stimulate thinking about superstition, Christian philosophy and state welfare. The reader will likely hate it or love it passionately. Passion on either side will indicate that these topics are important to the reader. I believe that they are not just important but critical to freedom, individual rights and to happiness.

The reader and I will make this journey together. I use the term "we" throughout the text as you and I examine and critique scripture, and as we draw our conclusions from that examination. I hope that when the reader is finished with the book he will reclaim any part of his life and money that he has previously given to the peddlers of superstition. Equally important, I hope that he will be able to state his claim to his own money that is presently being confiscated by the peddlers of altruism.

I refer to mankind and womankind as "man". I realize that doing so might be a distraction to some, but it makes for easier writing and reading. I hope that this approach is not offensive. It is not my intent to place women or womankind in any kind of inferior position. The Bible incorrectly does that. There is no difference at all between man and woman within the context and meaning of this work. The circumstances and actions of men in this book apply equally to those of women.

None of the arguments herein pertain to any particular religious denomination; therefore the term "priest" is used in a generic sense throughout the text to denote the leader of any organized religion.

PART I

What is Religion?

CHRONOLOGY

"Nothing is clearer than the fact that primitive man, whether in New Guinea today or eons ago in the prehistoric wilderness, is not and never has been a creature who peoples his world with bright fancies and lovely visions. Horrors lurked in the primeval forest, not nymphs and naiads. Terror lived there, with its close attendant, Magic, and its most common defense, Human Sacrifice. Mankind's chief hope of escaping the wrath of whatever divinities were then abroad lay in some magical rite, senseless but powerful, or in some offering made at the cost of pain and grief." (1)

Primitive man lived in a dangerous world where he was at the mercy of the elements that he had no understanding of. He knew that beasts, wind, lightning; torrential rain, volcanoes or earthquakes threatened his very existence almost continually. Assuredly he looked for explanations for the array of circumstances that he dreaded. His explanations almost always led to demons of one sort or another: ugly, horrifying creatures that seemed capable of and willing to destroy him at any time and without notice. He warned his children of the demons, and related his experiences with them. He looked for ways to appease them believing that they had a rational mind like his own. When some particular appeasement seemed to work, it became magic. He passed that knowledge on to his children as well. Whole systems of magic were developed over the years of those primitive societies that were able to survive their tormentor's attacks.

Obviously the magic didn't always work. Another member of the tribe tried a different approach, and it appeared to ward off the evil or to get some desired result. This was more powerful magic. The new man of magic, the medicine man, the witchdoctor, earns prestige with his power. He is either called on to lead the tribe, or he is hired on as the chief's personal medicine man. He is one to be admired for his power over the elements. He becomes an icon of both power and fear among his fellows: power for what he can do to ward off destruction, and fear that he might abandon his tribe or turn his magic against any one or all of them. They court the pleasure of the magic man: this strange, powerful man who can ward off evil.

Man's existence changed dramatically over the years. He acquired some knowledge of the elements. He systemized the production of his needs. He became a herdsman or a farmer. He made better weapons to both protect himself and to hunt with. The powerful acquired slaves to supply their needs so that they had time to pursue something beyond bare existence. One of the things they now had time to do was to just think. They thought mostly about how to retain their power, and what they knew was that force and magic were two inseparable elements for doing so. These men of the sword and magic were very powerful. Their tribes were small at first, but they expanded their domains by bloody conquest and fear. Their heirs would be given the secrets of power and be known as kings. The heirs of their medicine men would be given the secrets of the mysteries of magic and be known as priests.

The powerful men of Greece enjoyed a life of indulgence, and they had lost to some degree their fear of supernatural elements. They invented gods of a different type. Their gods were created by poets and in the image of man. To a large degree their gods suffered from some of the same interpersonal conflicts that their lessor earthly counterparts did. Many of them lived in the clouds of heaven. They were to be feared because they were very powerful and dangerous, but men could be relatively comfortable with them if they acted properly.

WESTERN RELIGIONS

Jewish tradition goes back to the Creation and the advent of Adam. Doctrine puts that date at about 4004 BC. In chapter 3 of the New Testament, Luke records 74 generations between the Creation and the birth of Jesus. However, since Adam and his immediate descendants could not have had any literary skills, it's impossible to assume that Luke's genealogy account is accurate. Even assuming that the genealogy is accurate, the placement of Adam in time still leaves the problem of the age of the parent at the time of procreation. If that average age is twenty years, Adam originated about 1480 BC. The average age of procreation would have to be fifty-four years in order to place the Creation at 4004 BC. That is highly unlikely in spite of the proposition that some of these men lived to be hundreds of years old.

It's generally believed that the seven-day calendar was the invention of the Samaritans and was adopted by the Jews. Since seven days are central to Genesis, we must assume that the invention of Adam followed the early Samaritans and early Greek mythology. The Jews created man in God's image by reversing what the Greek poets had done.

Religious and philosophical thinking in the Far East would also predate Adam. It was largely the product of the ruling and priestly classes. That thinking concerned itself with Man's physical and psychological condition. Some of it dealt with the futility of Man's existence, and some of it dealt with a right way of living. We see evidence of both in Old Testament doctrine.

The Catholic was the first institutionalized Christian church. It is commonly referred to as the Roman Catholic Church because its center is at the see of Rome. Its head is in the bishop of Rome who is designated as Pope, and its origin was during the declining years of the Roman Empire. Its doctrine comes from the Holy Bible. The Pope is believed to be the Vicar of Christ.

Mohammed was born about the close of the sixth century. He taught that there were thousands of prophets, but that six of them have precedence. They are Adam, Noah, Abraham, Moses, Jesus and Mohammed. Each brought new laws or dispensations, which successively abrogated the preceding ones. He taught that man's destiny is preordained, and that all good or evil comes from Divine will.

The Greek Orthodox was the first split with the Roman Catholic Church. It occurred during the middle of the ninth century. It disavows the authority of the Pope, and it asserts that the Church of Rome is not the true Catholic Church.

Martin Luther's split with the Roman Church began in the first quarter of the sixteenth century when he posted his ninety-five theses on the Castle Church of Wittenberg, Germany. The Lutheran Church bears his name. It was among the first of a multitude of Protestant religions, all of which formed a new version of its parent due to dissent over points of doctrine or organization. These spin-offs are essentially the same as Mohammed's doctrine of new dispensations replacing previous doctrine.

At this juncture, the reader should ask himself if he believes that supernatural demons actually lurked in the primeval forests. If so, you should save yourself the trouble of reading any further. The same question applies to belief in the supernatural gods of the Greeks. Read on only if those supernatural demons and supernatural gods are obviously myths and the inventions of man's mind. Since the supernatural is central to the concept of all gods, we can proceed with reasonable hope of establishing that the supernatural god, Jehovah, is of the exact same genre. He is an invention of man's mind. He is the supernatural in man's image.

SWORDS AND TEMPLES

Kings and priests have lived in a state of mutual dependency and mutual distrust ever since the first witchdoctor performed a miracle. Ever since that time, the king has needed the blessing of the priest, and thus the favor of the masses, to wield the power of the sword. The king also needed the obedience of the masses. He didn't attain it by any argument for justice, but by claiming the divine origin of his throne and that of the state. The priest was there to assure the masses that the king did indeed have a divine right to his throne. The priest has forever needed the power of the sword that he cannot wield to put more food and other niceties on his table. But the priest has generally had the upper hand due to his power over the minds of his subjects. The kings then have found it necessary to court the favor of the priests, or in some cases they have chosen to hire a different priest, in order that they could maintain and/or expand their power.

Rulers by association with divinity or pureness could reaffirm their right to rule and the right of their descendants to rule.

> "From him was descended the virgin Alang Goa, who conceived a miraculous child without a father, whose descendent in the tenth generation was Jenghiz Khan. The Mongols, brothers of the Turks, are thus the descendents of Gray Wolf, and their royal family derives its origin from the virgin who conceived a son without sin."(2)

Alang Goa had three other sons by virtue of miraculous conceptions after the death of her husband.

Prince Wladislaw III of Poland was disposed to seek the blessing of the Pope to assure the noble class of Poland that he was deserving of the crown. After defeating the Teutonic knights who had fallen out of favor with the Pope, he...

> "had it now in his power to exterminate the order; but, at the sacrifice of policy, he contented himself with taking possession of his own territory, and binding them down by a treaty.
>
> "Having thus fought the battles of his country, he returned, to obtain the crown which his subjects could no longer refuse. However, to give the ceremony the sanction of religion, Wladislaw sent an ambassador to Rome, to persuade the pope, more perhaps by a liberal sum of money than words, to ratify it with his authority.

> This confirmation being obtained, the ceremony of coronation was performed with great pomp in the cathedral at Cracow."(3)

Boris of Bulgaria attained the throne in 852.

> "Boris realized that Christianity was indispensable if he wanted to maintain his kingdom among powerful Christian neighbors—Franks, Moravians, and Byzantines. The Slavs of Thrace and Macedonia had already for the most part thrown off heathendom, and even in Boris' own realm Christianity had begun to strike deep roots ever since the time of Crum. Boris accepted Christianity for political reasons, just as the Russian Vladimir and the Magyar Stephen did later."(4)

European history is replete with intrigue and deals between various princes and the religious powers. The preceding are but a tiny example.

The reformation, the biggest split with the Roman Church, was about money and politics, both of which are the bridesmaids of religions, and both of which provide strong religious motivation. It could be argued that Martin Luther's intentions were purely philosophical, and that his purpose for challenging Pope Leo X and the practice of selling indulgences was as he said, "Out of love for the truth...." It would be generous to concede to that argument. There is little doubt that money and politics drove the success of the reformation, and there is no reason to believe that Luther's motivation was purely religious and philosophical.

> "What combination of forces and circumstances enabled nascent Protestantism to survive the hostility of both papacy and Empire? Mystical piety, Biblical studies, religious reform, intellectual development, Luther's audacity, were not enough; they might have been diverted or controlled. Probably the economic factors were decisive: the desire to keep German wealth in Germany, to free Germany from papal or Italian domination, to transfer ecclesiastical property to secular uses, to repel Imperial encroachments upon the territorial, judicial, and financial authority of the German princes,

cities, and states. Add certain political conditions that permitted the Protestant success."(5)

Mortals *invented* all religions. The first gods were conjured from the imaginations of witch doctors. Their characteristics are evident in pre-Greek art, monuments and other artifacts. Variations of these god-demons seem to be universal, and were witnessed by the European explorers in virtually every culture that they encountered. The Greek poets didn't invent religions, but they invented the man-like gods who resided in the heavens. The Greek concept of man-like, heavenly gods provided the basis for the god invented by the Jews. All western religions follow that model. They didn't come from divine revelation. Men invented religions to suit their needs for control and power.

ANTI-MIND & ANTI-MAN

Religions are essentially anti-man: particularly those that expound original sin. They, in fact, make no pretence otherwise. The cornerstone of western religions is the doctrine that man is imperfect and lowly in the eyes of the god that created him. When man is held up and compared to this god, he must be ashamed of his very existence. The more shame that he feels, and the more humble and unworthy he can make himself, the worthier he becomes in the eyes of his god. But there is no bottom to be reached. Lowliness is infinite. A man cannot debase himself enough to ever feel worthy.

> "The Desert Fathers realized that the most dangerous activity of the devil came into play against the monk only when he was morally perfect, that is, apparently 'pure' and virtuous enough to be capable of spiritual pride. Then began the struggle with the last and subtlest of the attachments: the attachment to one's own spiritual excellence; the love of one's spiritualized, purified and 'empty' self; the narcissism of the perfect, of the pseudo-saint and of the false mystic."(6)

We're talking here about monks who spend their entire lives attempting to reach a point where they might be worthy. But as we see, the monk hasn't a chance. So what chance does the average, normal man have? There is no chance for man to like himself, but he has one opportunity to please this god. He can beg for forgiveness. He can bow his head and get down on his knees or prostrate himself on the ground and beg forgiveness for his unworthy being. Pride of any kind is anathema. If a man happens to accomplish anything deemed worthy of praise by others, he must give the credit to his god.

It's important to recognize that the preceding quote came from a man, and it is about ideas that came from men, not from a supernatural being. It's included here because it is a perfect example of the goal and one of the tools of religion. The goal is to control the mind of man because mind control is the acme of power. One excellent way to control a man's mind is to continually reinforce the notion that he is unworthy or inferior, and then to offer him forgiveness or succor.

Life itself is thus denigrated. This is the same life that is valued by "Thou shalt not kill". But what is the value of a life that cannot be enjoyed? Life without joy has no value to itself. Many religious people will argue that religion doesn't prevent them from being happy. Many will in fact argue that religion actually enhances happiness: that their religion and their relationship with their god is the source of happiness itself. That happiness is based upon the myth that they are going to be the beneficiaries of some perfect existence in *the next life*. That alleged happiness is based on denial of this life and hope for another life that doesn't exist. It's a denial of their mortality. It's denial of who they really are. It's a visit to the unreal, to illusion. It's essentially the same as the escape from this life that one gets from smoking pot.

The anti-man nature of religions is also manifest in the concept of sacrifice. Christian religions hold up the supreme "sacrifice" of Jesus as a model, and from that context, any sacrifice that man is asked to make is viewed as a mere pittance, puny when compared to that of Jesus: not a real sacrifice at all. Foremost is the sacrifice of wealth to the church. A tithe is considered appropriate, but if we don't always feel that we can afford that much, no small sacrifice is turned down. Some religions do however require a tithe in order to participate in certain rituals of the religion. That means that if we want to be a real member of the church, we need to dig deeper into our pockets than we are comfortable doing. Sacrifice and discomfort are perfect companions.

Sacrifice doesn't end with cash for the church. It often includes our time. Since our time and our life mean essentially the same thing, this sacrifice of time is about sacrificing part of our life. Consider the impact of the Sabbath day. To dedicate one day to rest and to attend church is to give up fourteen percent of our life. There is nothing wrong with resting the body and brain for a day if we choose to do so. But to feel obliged to not do any kind of work for one day each week, at least not any that the neighbors might see, in order to please a mandate from a god, is being robbed of that part of our lives. If we add that loss of time to paying a tithe, we can actually be robbed of twenty four percent of our lives if we are good Christians. Imagine what we could add to our personal lives if we were not asked to make that sacrifice in the name of religion.

The time and money of its members is the lifeblood of religions. Without *our* time and *our* money, all religions would wither away. There would be no priests parading about in fine robes, and there would be no fine ornate buildings for them to parade in. There would be no wine to sip from a silver chalice that wouldn't exist either. Like their subjects, these showmen would be required to go to work every day, and they would have to be satisfied with the mundane existence of a human. This entire costly show is supported by three simple concepts: fear, guilt and hope.

As if owning one fourth of our lives isn't enough, we're also told how to spend much of the balance of it. Controlling lifestyles includes defining makeup, diet, literature, recreation, attire, wealth distribution, sex roles, male and/or female circumcision and a myriad of things that fall between these extremes are within the domain of religious control.

All religions don't attempt to give direction for all life choices. Each has its own set of priorities that determine the nature and amount of lifestyle direction given. What they all seek to control is the mind, and that gives them power over the man. Lifestyle control is simply an extra vehicle for mind control. Religion is about control, not freedom and not happiness.

What are we told when we question religious dogma? What are we told when we can't make sense of it? We are attacked. The anti-man face of religion tells us that this god works in strange ways. It tells us that our evil little brain isn't capable of understanding this god. We are told that we are so consumed by our petty little desires that we are blind to the truth. We are told that we are so wrapped up in the sins of this world that we have lost our faith. Being anti-mind is the essence of being anti-man because the mind is the only thing that separates us from our animal cousins. Some religious leaders tell us that our mind is at the core of our imperfection, and they chastise men who think. Carlstadt, a theologian at Wittenberg, "proclaimed that schools and studies were deterrents to piety, and that real Christians would shun all letters and learning, and would become illiterate peasants or artisans."(7) He was right when he suggested that knowledge is a deterrent to piety. He could have added that it is the enemy of faith.

Religions must be authoritarian because they must totally support their own myths. To tolerate any criticism or questions of the myth would be to invite their own destruction because the myth is the philosophical center of the religion. Since the myth is alleged to be from divine inspiration, it must be defended at all costs. To amend the myth is tantamount to challenging divine inspiration. If the philosophical center were allowed to develop any cracks, it wouldn't take long for the entire myth to collapse. The result is that religions are forced to punish dissidents. Whether the dissident is questioning some aspect of the myth or the authority of the religion, the religion cannot respond with debate, it must respond with punishment. Excommunication is normally the extreme punishment of our time, however death was common in the past, and we know of at least one death that was ordered during the 1980's. It is not outside the pale of reason to assume that there were others.

SILENT

History reveals more silence than protest from religions on key moral issues within the public arena. We earlier discussed the dependence of political leaders upon the authority of religious sanction. It is just as common for religious leaders to ignore the immoral actions of the ruler or ruling class. Religions don't want to antagonize a powerful leader or rankle too many of their constituents that have a popular agenda. They will avoid doing so if they can, because the moral choice could lead to the loss of member support. So given the unhappy choice of popularity or morality, popularity often wins out. The delicate way to deal with the problem is to ignore it. In addition, it is not uncommon for the priest to be in bed politically with the king.

The issue of slavery is at least as old as the Old Testament. The discussion about dealing with servants in chapter 21 of Exodus is not a discussion about how to deal with paid servants. It's about dealing with servants in bondage. These people were owned and discussed in the same manner that cattle were discussed. There wasn't even an issue of controversy at the time, but the condition existed. Their god apparently had no problem with slavery. Martin Luther supported it as follows.

> "The 'freedom of the Christian man' was to be understood as a spiritual liberty, consistent with serfdom, even with slavery."(8)
> "Did not Abraham and other patriarchs and prophets use slaves? Read what St. Paul teaches about servants, who at that time were all slaves. Therefore your third article is dead against the Gospel....This article would make all men equal....and that is impossible. For a worldly kingdom cannot stand unless there is in it an

inequality of persons, so that some are free, some imprisoned, some lords, some subjects."(9)

The position of religious leaders on slavery has generally been consistent with the political leaders of their time, and the same is generally true of many "value" issues. The latter years of slavery in America saw criticism or support from religions depending upon the geography of the religion. They took the popular high ground, not the moral high ground. If the Bible were inspired by a god as Paul would have us believe, it's interesting that this god never criticized the immoral practice of servitude.

During the fifteenth century one in five Christian male children became the property of Muhammed II within all of the provinces of his empire. It was declared that such was the lawful price of toleration to those who refused to embrace Islam. While one religion might have objected to this practice the other one obviously did not. Right for one religion was wrong for the other. The same is true of the crusades which found the Pope in total support of bloody wars that were intended to wrestle the Holy Land from Moslem control. The Catholics and Protestants murder each other in Ireland, and Central Europe is an ethnic (politically correct term for religious) slaughterhouse. Some religious leaders might call for peace or a peaceful settlement, but we don't hear any of them telling their particular constituents to walk away from their particular dogma.

Christians have persecuted the Jews for two thousand years. Have we heard anything of substance from the Christian leadership that would possibly put an end to it? No. The "witches" of Europe and New England were tortured and burned at the hands of religious zealots, and their leaders were either silent or co-conspirators. Hitler and a host of other assassins have been blessed with the silence of religious leaders. Silence on divisive moral issues has historically been the norm of religious leadership. Fortunately there is no hell because if there was one, many religious leaders would most assuredly be burning there for their crimes against man, and for their silence in the presence of murderers.

DIVISIVE

"Glory to God in the highest, and on earth 'peace,' good will toward men." Luke, 2:14.
"Suppose ye that I am come to give peace on earth? I tell you, Nay; but rather division:" Luke, 12:51.

The latter has proved to be true. Religions foster ethnocentricity, tribalism. It is their nature to do so. Is it possible to even imagine the leader of any religion to say that his superstition is no better than any other superstition? Of course it's not. He must assert the rightness of his superstition. To do otherwise would destroy the myth that supports his particular mysteries. When the myth is destroyed, the religion disappears. This dogmatic clinging to the "true" myth is at the core of ethnic hate and violence. History is filled with its evidence and its tragic, bloody result.

These are the more obvious displays of tribal hate, but tribal hate is not limited to just the obviously violent areas of the world. In America where religious freedom is a constitutional guarantee, the divisiveness is subtler, but it is just as prevalent. We see it in letters to the editors, we see it on the Internet, and we hear it at thousands of water cooler discussions. Parents admonish their children to make friends with the "right" kids and not to spend too much time with "those others". Parents pass on their distrusts and dislikes to their children who in turn pass them on to their own. These subtle dislikes are semi-transparent in the workplace, in the classroom and on the athletic field, but in the real lives of these people, at the core, divisiveness is there. For some it's just a nagging little question as to whether the other is all right. For some it's a dominant negative factor in their view of the other. It might never manifest itself outwardly, but it's there. The division is there because his superstition is the true one. His tribe is the right one. If push comes to shove, the violence will be there too.

Religion is not about joy to the world and peace on earth. The ancient and modern history of religion is about distrust, hate, torture and blood. That will never change because the nature of religion cannot change. The insistence that my superstition is the right superstition is the nucleus of tribal hate. It's somewhat amazing that all of the misery caused by religion is the result of ancient superstition: belief in the supernatural.

BIG BUSINESS

Religion is the largest single industry on the planet with the possible exception of the production and distribution of food. In addition to the direct collection of billions of dollar equivalents in dues that are untaxed, many religions are direct owners of some businesses and/or they are stockholders of publicly traded companies. Since religions operate free from any scrutiny by any government or any government agency, there is no way to even guess at how vast the wealth of some religions is, although some are obviously extremely wealthy. There is nothing categorically wrong with that. There is nothing wrong with wealth even if scripture does tell us that it (money) is filthy. If there were an issue at all, it would be concerning what is done with all of that wealth.

John the Baptist said, "He that hath two coats, let him impart to him that hath none; and he that hath meat, let him do likewise". It would seem reasonable then that those religions that enjoy great wealth would first heed the word of John. They could alleviate, if not eliminate, the poverty of their followers. Those religions that choose to use their wealth to expand their domain rather than to relieve the suffering of their own, would seem to be out of step with the altruism which the New Testament so strongly advocates. Perhaps like their god, religions work in strange ways too. Yet it might be more consistent with doctrine than it first appears. Religions claim to be interested in saving souls, not lives. It would also be consistent with the anti-man philosophy. So it might be that John's altruistic mandate applies only to individual members of the church but not to the church itself. That perhaps justifies sacrifice of the individual and expansion of the church.

The advent of television ushered in a new format for selling religion on a grand scale. It provided a new medium whereby preachers could reach a massive audience, and the televangelists have done exactly that. These preachers may or may not be sectarian, but they have identical goals: to reach the largest possible audience, and to appear to be like a friendly, approachable counselor as well as a preacher. If acquiring vast fortunes is a measure of success, some of them have been extremely successful. Where does all of that money go?

There is also a flourishing industry that operates independently of religions, but it thrives upon religious doctrine. This is the publishing and music industry. Here we find periodicals and books on every imaginable religious topic and attempting to appeal to every variety of religious and mystic interests. On the conservative side we have attempts to verify elemental doctrine. On the exotic side we have novelists pouring forth their imaginings of the rapture. Recording artists are also benefactors of the religious myths. Some thrive on gospel music, and many record a Christmas carol or two. This is both business and art. The benefactors are the publishing houses and the artists. We're not concerned with their motives. They simply add to the vast amount of wealth that revolves around religion.

RELIGION OR CULT

New religions have a way of just showing up from time to time. Some of these have been in the form of spin-offs from existing religions where a dissident perhaps takes issue with some point of doctrine or practice. He invents a doctrine or practice that is more suitable to him. He manages to attract some people who agree with him, and we have a new religion. Established religions, however, would prefer to call this new group a cult or a sect because those terms lack the moral authority that is associated with "religion". The Protestant split with Rome had the immediate support of the state so a new "religion" came into being as soon as the state declared it so. The Mormons were referred to as a sect late into the twentieth century. They are now numerous and wealthy and thereby apparently deserve the ranking of a religion.

New religions (sects) continue to show up. Their doctrine and practices can be secretive and/or bizarre, or they may just seem that way to established religious thinking. They are almost always viewed with suspicion by the public at large, the press and government authorities. Some have met tragic fates at their own hands or the hands of the authorities. Many thought that when the Heaven's Gate cult committed suicide that it was a tragic event. Others suggest that it was the natural outcome for a group that was earnestly seeking a higher consciousness, and that is what most religions do. They just don't do it with the same level of intensity. But the fact remains that there is no essential difference between cults or religions. They all have a negative view of man's condition, and they all have a formula whereby he can improve it. Perhaps the Heavens Gate cult is less tragic than some imagined. They attained nirvana. Isn't that what other religions are selling?

The motivation of those who started new religions comes into question. Were they truly motivated by the desire to provide the "right" or "true" religion for man, or was their motivation of a more personal and selfish nature? There have always been substantial benefits for the leaders of a religion. They have power over the minds and thus over the pocketbooks of their followers. They have the power to implement practices that provide physical and psychological benefits for themselves. We can only imagine what it would be like to have a couple hundred faithful followers that were willing to donate a tithe to the new religion. That would indeed be quite comfortable.

THE FISH AND THE FORMULA

"And Jesus said unto Simon, Fear not: from henceforth thou shalt catch men." Luke, 5:10.

Man has searched for meaning since before the beginning of recorded history. The apparent futility of existence seems to be more than he can bear. There must be some meaning beyond that which he can see. He needs a higher meaning. This life is pointless to him. He needs a reason for his existence, something to believe in, something beyond birth, maturity, reproduction and death. This life is not enough for him. His stature in life is not good enough for him. He needs to be special. He deserves to sit at the table next to the king. He is willing to deceive himself with virtually any notion that will rescue him from his pedestrian existence.

Religion gives man that special meaning. It lifts him up from his mediocrity. It tells him that he is special, that his god, the king of kings, has a special interest in him. It assures him that this life is indeed futile, but not to despair because his god has prepared a special place for him in one of his heavenly mansions. All that he need do is to maintain his faith in the face of the evil temptations that he experiences in this life. His faith will conquer evil. His faith will reap the reward that he so desperately desires. He is special. He will find higher meaning. He will sit next to the king.

Catching men is not too difficult. Ideally they are caught by parents that were caught by their parents that were caught by their parents that just happened to grow up under a king that had made a deal with a specific priest. Most of the men who descended from any particular state inherited a religious identity as well as a national identity. Many that immigrated to a different nation gradually gave up their original national identity, but they retained their religious identity, and they passed it on to virtually every succeeding generation. So the bulk of men are caught by their ancestors and simply handed over to a religion. It is only a small minority of men that have taken the trouble to challenge the religion that was forced on their ancestors by some prince or king that they know absolutely nothing about.

Religions do some active catching as well. They train some of their followers in the basic myths of the religion, and send them out to catch men. They cast their nets into a large pond filled with many men. They are almost certain to catch a few that are looking for that higher meaning but who haven't made a conscious effort to find it. Now a full-blown myth is handed to them, and it provides them with that nebulous something that will add a meaning to their life that wasn't there before.

There will likely be a few men in the pond that have been brought up under a religious system that they question. There might be some tenets or practices that don't fit their needs or mindsets. The myth from the fisherman of men feels better to them than the myth that they inherited. The new myth gives them that something that they were looking for. It just seems to fit better.

But the business of religion isn't complete in the process of catching men. It must keep them in the net as well. Men must continue to feel good about their religion. Each religion has its own formula to accomplish this, but there are basic similarities that are centered on the Sabbath day. Once each week the followers are rescued from the drudgery of everyday life and transported to a special world of reassurance, music and tribal unity. This is powerful magic.

The meeting of the congregation takes on a special meaning because the members treat it as special. They wear their very best clothing. Many have clothing so special that it is only worn on this occasion. They also put on their very best demeanor. Some perform a regular ritual of greeting others before entering the place of worship where they can hopefully take their position in the same place that they have always taken for as far back as they can remember. This isn't absolutely necessary, but it adds to their level of comfort if they are able to occupy the same position adjacent to those that they have always positioned themselves by. For some there might be a subtle, unspoken bonding in this, for others it's as basic as being in their comfort zone.

The services are as varied as the religions are, and in some cases as varied as the congregations are. All have a ritual of some kind to reinforce the power of the myth. The ritual includes one or more messages from their god along with a vehicle that is unique to the particular religion for presenting the message. The vehicle with which the message is presented is as important as the message itself. The message can be a reminder to man of his base nature, a reminder of the power and grace of the god, or a combination of both. The basic myth is confirmed subtly or boldly depending upon variables of the religious calendar, local events and national or international politics. Virtually any circumstance is capable of reinforcing the myth if the circumstance is in the hands of a deft speaker.

The final key ingredient of the formula is music: motivational, powerful music. Whether it's performed by a pretty good volunteer choir, a soloist, or by the congregation, religious music plays a major role in making that religious meeting very special. Some of that music is very good, and most religious people have one or two favorite compositions that turn a good service into a very special one. Standing in the church next to people that they are comfortable with and singing a favorite hymn to the best of their ability is a powerful bonding experience. The combination of the shared myth and the shared music provides very powerful glue for the tribe. The last hymn of the service can stay on their lips, or at least in their minds, until the day ends. Thereby the myth can stay with them and provide that uplifting thing and a sense of belonging that they need right into their dreams of the night. The men have not only been caught; they are euphoric about their captivity.

They know that there are doubters in the world. They have doubts of their own at times. They look into the faces of their fellow worshipers and wonder if they really believe this stuff? "Of course they do", they reason. "They wouldn't be here if they didn't. But I'm here, and sometimes I'm not so sure. Should I ask them? No. I couldn't. I couldn't admit to any lack of faith. I must have faith. They have faith. Yes, of course, they believe. How could I ever question that?"

Most of the faithful have limited knowledge of their religion, and they know even less about religion in general. A small minority has read scripture, and who could blame those who haven't for not doing so? Most who have read scripture just read it. They read it in the same way that they read a novel, a gigantic adventure story. In many ways that is exactly what it is. They just absorb the words without examining what they mean, and without questioning their credibility. Those who do question it and who trust their own mind must surely walk away from it. Fortunately for religions, the latter is a miniscule minority. The Papal see prohibited the general reading of the Bible for several centuries. The Pope quite likely had concern that general reading of the Bible would lead to disbelief. There was little to fear. Men didn't, and still don't, take the time to do any serious study or critique of the Bible.

What about those fishermen of men; why are they attracted to "the cloth"? Is it possible that many of them realize that it's much easier to take fish from those who catch them than it is to catch their own?

CREDIT

Some religions operate excellent schools. They devote time to the study of their particular myth, but their primary focus is to provide a good education to the children of the congregation. These schools are commonly the envy of public schools that operate in the same geographical area. They will normally admit non-congregation children into their classrooms when student space permits, and this outside demand often exceeds the capabilities of the school even though non-member parents are required to pay extra for the schooling. These schools deserve due credit for the quality of the education that they provide and for the example they set for most public schools.

Although done within the wrong context, religions provide to varying degrees what little support remains for the commandments. Moral guidelines are essential to healthy human relationships, and the commandments of a god provide those guidelines to those people who are incapable of defining morality in any other terms. We will see in Part VII that some of the commandments are essential to the survival of civilization and to man's individual happiness. To the extent that religions have upheld those particular commandments to their followers, they have helped to slow the process of moral decay, which if unchecked, will destroy civil relationships.

Many religions respond with various types of humanitarian aid to disaster stricken areas of the world. Some also help to provide for the needy within their own communities. Some have regular programs to assist people within their community to get off welfare and to become self-sufficient, and some have a variety of helping hand programs. These programs are of tremendous value to their recipients, and when viewed alongside the religious schools and religious support of moral values, religions appear to be a value to society as a whole. But when we look at the total impact of religions upon the total of society, we recognize that these few benefits to society are few and small when compared to just the evil of divisiveness that is inherent in religion.

PART II

Reason vs. Non-reason

In parts III and IV we will closely examine parts of the Bible. We will observe countless discrepancies within the text itself and with our own knowledge of certain facts. This in itself is quite easy for anyone to do. The difficulty arises from the fact that the adversaries of reason, the advocates of faith, tell us that logic and our power of reasoning are insufficient to challenge the word of this god. Our task then in this section is to validate the reasoning power of man.

ACCEPTING THE ABSURD

We encounter numerous believers or keepers of the faith who are unwilling to even entertain the possibility that scripture is in any way faulty. Their faith is total, complete, and unquestionable. They will not even consider a challenge to the words of the Bible. They may or may not recognize the contradictions within the text and/or the contradictions with their own perception of reality. Neither matters to them. They have no problem denying their own capacity to challenge the contradictions. They have no problem denying their own reasoning power. The elasticity of their minds permits them to put square pegs into round holes. The facts of reality can contradict the facts of scripture without creating a problem for them. They have two realities. The first is the reality of their cognition. The second is the reality of miracles and faith. In any contest between faith and their own cognition, their cognition is sacrificed to faith.

"Intellectually speaking, the period of the Middle Ages was the exact opposite of classical Greece. Its leading philosophic spokesman, Augustine, held that faith was the basis of man's entire mental life. 'I do not know in order to believe,' he said, 'I believe in order to know.' In other words, reason is nothing but a handmaiden of revelation; it is a mere adjunct of faith, whose task is to clarify, as far as possible, the dogmas of religion. What if a dogma cannot be clarified? So much the better, answered an earlier Church father, Tertullian. The religious man, he said, delights in thwarting his reason; that shows his commitment to faith. Thus Tertullian's famous answer, when asked about the dogma of God's self-sacrifice on the cross: 'Credo quia absurdum' ('I believe it because it is absurd').(1)

Martin Luther informs us that we cannot accept both the Bible and reason. One or the other must go.

"All the articles of our Christian faith, which God has revealed to us in His Word, are in presence of reason sheerly impossible, absurd, and false. What (thinks that cunning little fool) can be more absurd and impossible than that Christ should give us in the Last Supper His body and Blood to eat and drink?...or that the dead should rise again at the last day?_or that Christ the Son of God should be conceived, borne in the womb of the Virgin Mary, become man, suffer, and die a shameful death on the cross?...Reason is the greatest enemy that faith has....She is the Devil's greatest whore...a whore eaten by scab and leprosy, who ought to be trodden underfoot and destroyed, she and her wisdom...Throw dung in her face...drown her in baptism."(2)

"All the articles of our Christian faith, which God has revealed to us in His Word, are in presence of reason sheerly impossible, absurd, and false." "Reason is the greatest enemy that faith has." Those are two powerful and telling statements, and Luther is totally correct. What he would have us do is not. To deny one's reason in favor of superstition is as absurd as all the articles of Christian faith. Luther preferred superstition to reason, and he would have us do the same. If we do that, we might as well resume the practice of sacrificing young virgins to the volcano.

It's important to examine Luther's abusive harangue of reason because it's typical of the religious argument against reason. He is absolutely correct when he states that reason is the greatest enemy of faith because there is no possible way to reconcile the two. It's interesting that faith's greatest enemy is mans greatest asset. Reason is mans primary means of survival. It's doubtful that mankind would have survived without it during the early stages of his existence because without it, he was no match for his animal cousins that would assuredly have enjoyed slaughtering and devouring him. Reason is the faculty that allows him to differentiate and to organize perceptual data in such a way that he can successfully exist. He is successful in relation to the degree that he can organize and integrate data accurately. Conversely, when his reason fails him, he is virtually helpless.

When Luther said that reason was the Devil's greatest whore, we must assume that his view of reason was that it had the same characteristics as a whore. In addition to being "for hire" those might include promiscuous, corrupt and unfaithful. Perhaps we can simply say that reason can be bought for a price because it has no scruples. The implication is that reason is willing to manipulate knowledge in order to come up with conclusions that are profitable for the moment. So the question is "Can reason be bought for a price?"

The senses perceive data, and the data is recorded in the mind. More perceptions send more data to the mind where it is recorded, and if it is consistent with previous data, it is integrated with the previous data. If the new data contradicts some previous data, the mind has to decide which seems to be accurate, the truth. After doing so, it will discard what it believes to be inaccurate, untrue. It builds up a store of what it believes to be accurate data over time, and that is its knowledge base. For example: square pegs only fit into square holes, and round pegs only fit into round holes, *never* visa versa. All of its actions are guided by its knowledge base because it believes that what it knows is accurate, the truth. A sane mind would find it impossible to *reason* that the round peg will fit into the square hole.

Luther would probably agree with us up to this point, but he might argue that reason could be bought for a price. Because reason is a whore, at least his reason, because that is the only reason he could know anything about, it will *believe* that the square peg will fit into the round hole if the price for believing it is right. She will believe it if it is to her advantage, and therefore reason cannot be trusted, at least not when it finds itself in a contradiction with faith.

That position is as absurd as he said were all of the articles of Christian faith when they were in the presence of reason. A sane, rational mind cannot deceive itself. It knows what it knows. No doubt there are things that it doesn't know, that if known, might adjust what it knows, but it cannot lie to itself. An irrational mind can lie to itself. It can attempt to hold contradictory concepts. That is precisely why it is irrational. If a rational mind is like a whore it's only when it denies its own reasoning, when it denies that which it knows. It is just being honest with itself when it refuses to accept the "sheerly impossible, absurd, and false."

Augustine, Tertullian and Luther had a mutual contempt for reason. Tertullian and Luther agreed that God's sacrifice of himself was absurd in the face of reason, and that they were willing to put their faith ahead of their own reason. Luther characterizes reason as the devil's greatest whore that ought to be trodden underfoot. It's important to note that all three of these men had to use their own reasoning powers to arrive at their particular position. Luther is telling us that we should accept his conclusions on the matter based upon his reasoning power. If we do that, we are simply negating our own ability to think for ourselves, and we are taking on faith that Luther's reasoning, that which he did not trust himself, was superior to our own. In effect, his reasoning power states that our reasoning power must be destroyed in order that we can accept the "sheerly impossible, absurd and false." To do that would be absurd.

Luther *knew* that the Bible was absurd. He *preferred* faith to reason; therefore it was necessary to attack reason. He had to denounce one or the other. Nobody will ever know why he made the choice that he did. Perhaps he truly believed that if his faith was strong enough that he too could defy the laws of physics and walk on water. Perhaps he was just another charlatan; eager to collect donations after the indulgences stopped going to Rome. Perhaps *his* reason was a whore. There is no justification for following his admonitions in any case.

To accept Luther's position is actually a cop-out: an excuse to escape the need to think. It's an excuse to accept his reasoning in order to avoid the hard work of doing our own thinking and reasoning. Thinking is difficult at times, particularly when attempting to reconcile conflicting data. So the believer who is confronted with his knowledge of his faith being contradicted by his cognition blindly accepts his faith rather than make the mental effort required to decide the validity of either. He actually does disservice to both in the process. He has not verified his faith by denying his cognition because denying his cognition is simply denial. Denial is a negative, a non-sum. It doesn't verify or affirm anything. He has simply determined that he doesn't trust his own mind. Therefore his faith is not faith by conviction, a positive, but faith by denial, a negative. He holds blind faith (the only kind there is) for the sake of maintaining it, not for the sake of determining what is true. He not only denies his own mind in this process; he denies his essence as a man, because man's mind is the essence of man. Without it man is just another animal that is the subject and victim of the whims of fate and the priest.

Using one's reason has one problem: it is hard work and difficult at times. This can be particularly true when one is faced with the task of discarding previously held knowledge when new information reveals a flaw in that knowledge. But if a man is to call himself a man, he must do the hard work of thinking that a man is required to do. He must attempt to discern what is true. If he is diligent and not mentally impaired, he is usually able to determine which of the contradictory data confronting him is true and which is false. His reward for that effort is confidence. The alternative is to follow like a sheep, to hold knowledge based upon faith and to set aside any data that contradicts it. He can just follow the herd to wherever it is going. This is surely the easier course. His reward for this lack of effort is whatever fate decides it will be.

Each man must decide for himself whether he can accept his own ability to think, or must he rely on the peddlers of superstition to do his thinking for him. There is no other alternative in this situation. Each man should be able to determine for himself whether his thought process is normally reliable. There is absolutely no reason for him not to trust it if it is. Knowing that his reasoning power is normally reliable, isn't it totally absurd to not trust it whenever it contradicts the absurd dialogue that allegedly came from some supernatural being? To believe that a supernatural power is able to reverse the laws of physics and nature is as absurd as believing in lucky socks. Both are equally absurd. If the reader believes in the power of lucky socks, black cats and broken mirrors, he should read no further.

PICK AND CHOOSE

Reporting on the Pope John Paul II visit to St. Louis, a reporter was seeking comments from admirers of the Pope. One woman was asked about her feelings regarding her religion. "I think you take the parts that fit with your life and struggle with the other parts", she replied. The Mormon Church makes a formal statement to the effect that they believe the Bible to be the word of God as far as it is translated correctly. Both statements reflect a selective belief. The St. Louis woman wants to buy the parts that fit with her lifestyle. The Mormons accept the parts that are translated correctly, but who can possibly know which parts those are. If somebody did know, it would seem reasonable to correct those parts that are in error. There is no way of knowing, of course, so the Mormons can kind of make up whatever fits their ideas of "right" religious doctrine.

The Mormons aren't alone in this regard. They just happen to make a formal statement to that effect. Each of the various Christian Religions has done the exact same thing. Somebody had a difference of opinion about doctrine or practice, and has turned that difference into a new religion. That is precisely why there are so many versions of Christianity. This has created a sort of potpourri of Christianity wherein each different religion adds its special scent. All of these variations are philosophical equivalents to the lady from St. Louis. They have taken the parts that they like and discarded the parts that they don't like, and they typically add a few twists of their own.

Our biblical source identified eighty-six variations of Christian churches at the time of publication in the year 1886. How can there be so many variations of Christianity? Jean Glapion, a Franciscan monk can give us a hint on that matter. He stated that "the Bible is like soft wax, which every man can twist and stretch according to his pleasure".(3) These are the words of a monk, and we must assume an apt student of the Bible. He was the confessor of the Emperor, Charles V. It seems that translation isn't the only problem with discovering the truth. The myth can be, and we can be certain that it is, twisted and stretched to the liking of whatever priest happens to be twisting and stretching it.

The fact that all of these religions call themselves Christian doesn't mean that they all call each other Christian. Most expound the general myth that Jesus was the Son of God. But for many, that is about as similar as they will admit to. Some even question if some others are worshipping the right Jesus. The other thing that they have in common is their selective form of dogma and practice. None of their arguments are based upon reason. Their differences are based upon personal preference, what the founder of their religion wanted them to believe. The faithful just follow.

Plato introduced the concept of higher truths. He alleged that these truths were only available to the intellectual elite, that the common man was incapable of grasping them. The priests incorporated this thinking into religious doctrine. Hence we have the doctrine that the god works in mysterious ways. This simple statement is meant to explain away all inconsistencies in scripture as well as the god's apparent lack of concern with the misfortune that is often inflicted upon his followers. The priests would have us believe that they know and understand the god, and that the god has a reason for everything regardless of how strange, absurd or brutal it might appear to the layman. The fact of the matter is that nobody, including the priests, knows anything about the god. They might be able to recite the Bible from memory: backward even, but they can't know anything about the god because there is no god to know.

Plato's "higher truths" and the god's "mysterious ways" are of the same genus. They hold up an elite few men as being uniquely able to comprehend the incomprehensible. That is of course a position that virtually any con man can assume. Anybody can dispense tons of garbage that isn't meant to be understood and then take the intellectual high ground by pretending to help the confused audience to understand the meaning of the garbage. The audience naturally feels inferior to the person who obviously understands the garbage, and they view him as exceptionally intelligent. He is conscious of "higher truths", or he understands the "mysteries". He becomes one who should be listened to because he comprehends the incomprehensible.

LOCKED IN

The final deterrent to making any intellectual challenge to scripture is the admonition to beware of false prophets. The message here is that anything that contradicts scripture is categorically false. The faithful consequently block out anything that contradicts scripture. They must block it out in order to avoid any challenge to their faith. Any challenge to scriptural teachings is automatically subject to doubt. By inventing the fear of false prophets the writers of the Bible effectively inhibited any challenge to its dogma by those that are victims of its myths. They are essentially slaves to a myth.

COGNITION OR MYSTICISM

In the process of examining scripture, it will become apparent that faith demands the denial of reason and reason demands the denial of faith. There can be no reconciliation of the two. Our fundamental question then is whether the mind has the capacity to think accurately, to know. Is it safe for the thinker to rely upon his own cognition in the process of evaluating the Bible? Stated another way, is cognition accurate and can it be trusted in this process?

Man's mind is what distinguishes him from his animal cousins. According to the Bible, man was given a free will. What that means is that man, unlike any other animal, has the ability to choose. He isn't locked into instinctive behavior, as are all other animals. The ability to make choices means that he has the ability to access any and all information that he has stored in his brain before taking action related to any circumstance. His ability to make good decisions and take appropriate action depends entirely upon the accuracy of the information that he has stored. Accurate information can also be referred to as true information, or the truth. His ability to survive depends entirely upon his ability to know the truth. How does he know the truth?

ACQUIRING AND VALIDATING KNOWLEDGE

The mind gathers information from the senses. Most information is gathered by the eyes and ears, and they relay the information to the mind where it is integrated with knowledge. Knowledge is previously gathered information that has been integrated with other information.

If the new information cannot be integrated with knowledge, if it creates a contradiction of some kind, the mind must evaluate the knowledge in comparison to the new information. It must, and normally does, decide which is true. If it makes the right decision, future decisions and actions will be based upon truer knowledge than they will be if the wrong decision is made. The process of assimilating data and integrating it with knowledge goes on as long as man lives and continues to take in new data. His success or failure rate at virtually everything he does depends upon the degree of truth of the knowledge that he holds.

This is largely a trial and error process that we can easily observe in young children. They attempt to put square pegs into round holes until their knowledge level reaches the point that such a thing would be absurd to them. They acquire data rapidly and attempt to integrate it with what they know. What they know changes almost as rapidly as they acquire new data. But if they work hard at learning what is true by integrating new data with their knowledge, their true knowledge expands, and the need for trial and error is diminished. The integration of new data with held knowledge is what we call "thinking". Thinking is the job of a rational mind. When a mind knows that the square peg will fit the round hole if it just tries one more time, it might lack experience. When a mind can't or won't think, when it accepts contradictions, when it believes that there is a trick, some mysterious way to fit the square peg into the round hole, it is irrational.

It is illogical to hold knowledge that square pegs will fit round holes. Logic means that our knowledge is non-contradictory. Round cannot be square in some situations, nor can blue be orange in some situations. Right is always right, and left is always left. A building cannot be an airplane, and a duck cannot be a horse. Logic is the result of accurate identification (a duck is a duck) and non-contradictory integration (ducks paddle in the water and fly in the sky, but you can't put a motor in a duck). Anything else is a contradiction. To maintain a contradiction is to deny the truth and to negate the mind. To negate the mind is to negate the essence of man.

"Free will", that thing that the god allegedly gave to man, is the ability to think rather than to be controlled and driven by instincts. The ability to think logically and without contradictions is a prerequisite to free will being of any value. Free will, without the ability to integrate data and think logically, is dangerous, as can be observed in the case of the mentally handicapped and deranged. Accurate identification, non-contradictory data, and logic are what make free will an asset rather than a hazard. If there was a god and he gave man a free will, he must also give him the tools, rationality and logic, in order to use it. Otherwise free will is dangerous or useless. If there was a fair and rational god, he could not give man inadequate tools of reason. Only a priest would do that.

WHO THINKS?

A normal mind has the freedom and the ability to think. It has the responsibility to think if it wants to remain free. It must acquire its own knowledge by doing its own job of integrating non-contradictory data. Knowing that it might error, it still must make its own decisions about what is true and what is false. It can correct any errors if more information becomes available.

The ability and willingness to know what is true based upon our own cognition is implicit in the concept of a free will. Otherwise a free will would be meaningless. Our personal knowledge of what is true is essential to the validation of our personal free will. Free will is not really free if the brain that operates it does not think for itself. Thinking demands the evaluation and integration of all available data. Integration of data demands that data that is contradictory to cognition be discarded. For free will to remain free, a mind cannot abdicate thinking to someone else. A mind that allows a king or a priest to do its thinking for it commits itself to slavery. Thomas Jefferson stated the case as follows.

> "...I never submitted the whole system of my opinions to the creed of any party of men whatever in religion, in philosophy, in politics, or in anything else where I was capable of thinking for myself. Such an addiction is the last degradation of a free and moral agent. If I could not go to heaven but with a party, I would not go there at all."(4)

Note that Jefferson refers to thinking as a moral obligation as well as the obligation of a free man. We should add that *critical thinking* is a moral obligation as well as that of a free man. This means that taking the word of the priest or the king without validating it with our own knowledge base is immoral and not worthy of a free man.

To do the work of thinking a mind must continually make choices in its attempt to integrate new data with its knowledge base. It must decide on its own if something is true or false, right or wrong. It must be willing to discard old knowledge or new data if one is in contradiction with the other. In doing so it must be honest with itself. It must be relentless in its effort to seek the truth. A mind cannot make moral decisions based upon the truth, if it is operating with contradictions, half-truths and/or falsehoods. Any mind that is willing to do the work of integrating non-contradictory data can think logically and with a high degree of accuracy. This can be hard work at times, but it is the only way that a mind can know the truth.

LOGIC AND MYSTERIES

We might admit that a rational mind is quite capable of integrating data, thinking logically and arriving at the truth, but it might still be incapable of understanding the mysterious ways of a god. To that we will indeed admit that yes, the god is too mysterious to be understood by a rational mind. But then we must ask why should that be so? If this god is responsible for our free will and the rational mind that is needed to operate it, why would he choose to be so mysterious that we can't understand him with that mind? If a god gave us free will and a rational mind, but that mind is incapable of understanding the one who gave it to us, then it's a bad gift. It's a curse. If we are confused by the contradictions of reason with the mysterious ways of the god, then the god is accountable for our confusion. Shame on the god for giving us a mind that can't understand him. There is absolutely no reason for it unless we are caught in some absurd game that we can't possibly win. What possible reason could there be for such a game? Why should there be any seeds of doubt at all?

The priest will tell us that man has an evil tendency about him: that his natural evil blinds him to the ways of the god. Indeed we are told in Genesis 6,5, that "God saw that the wickedness of man was great in the earth, and that every imagination of the thoughts of his heart was only evil continually." *Every imagination of man's mind* was continually evil. Isn't this the mind that the god gave to man? Didn't the god create man *just as he is*? He did indeed if he indeed created him. "Not so", says the priest. "Man has allowed Satan into his heart. Satan has blinded man to the truth". But if there is a Satan, the god knew of him. Surely he knew the power of Satan. Knowing the power of Satan, why did he make such a weak thing of man?

He was indeed disappointed with his creation. We learn in Genesis 6, verses 6,7 and 8 that the god was sorry for making man, and that he was prepared to destroy everything on earth as a result. "But Noah found grace in the eyes of the Lord". The result was that Noah and his three sons and their families were saved from the destruction of the earth. *But he didn't change the nature of man.* This omniscient, omnipotent god was naive enough to rewind the game and start over without changing the nature of man. He left man with the same mind and the same evil tendencies that he had previously. He was still too weak and blind to deal with the evil god, Satan. Man's mind, tempted by Satan or not, was still unable to understand the mysterious ways of the god. Free will and a rational mind remain a bad gift. Shame on the god.

Yet the priest still wants to rescue the god from his own dilemma. He tells us that if man had enough faith he wouldn't be confused. But how can this be if faith and reason are both products of the same mind? Is a mind to choose faith rather than its own reason, or is it to have faith in its own ability to decide what is true? If it cannot have confidence in itself then of what value is it? Life would just be one big continuous crapshoot if the mind couldn't have confidence in its own ability to know the truth. The god allegedly gave man the power of reasoning so that he would be able to choose between true and false, between right and wrong. Why is it then that man's reasoning power mysteriously becomes invalid when it contradicts faith? The answer to all of these questions is apparently just another mystery. There is one exception. It is not a mystery that faith demands the negation of the mind. Faith demands that the one characteristic that separates man from his animal cousins, his ability to think, must be ignored if it cannot reconcile itself with faith.

Man has had two masters throughout recorded history: the king and the priest. Man began his liberation from the king with The Declaration of Independence. That declaration gave man his first real opportunity at self-government. Most men have yet to be liberated from the priest, and a man is not truly free as long as the priest has control over his mind. No document or agreement with other men can do that for him. Each man must do that for himself. He must do it alone. He must decide for himself what is true and what is false. He must have confidence in his own mind that he can do so. The human mind, that wonderful device that gave man dominion over the earth, can know the truth, and it is the only thing that can free man from the priest.

THE BIBLE'S AUTHOR

The second book of Timothy, chapter 3, verse 16, tells us, "All scripture is given by inspiration of God, and is profitable for doctrine, for reproof, for correction, for instruction in righteousness:" This means that the god directed the writing of scripture at least until the time of Paul's epistle to Timothy. Therefore we should expect scripture to be totally accurate to that point. It seems reasonable that the god would continue to direct scriptural writing beyond that point as well, and that would also include all translations. To do less than that would constitute inexcusable negligence. If the Bible is to be used by man as a guide to righteousness, an omniscient, omnipotent god has the ability and duty to remove any possibility of error in terms of original and translated accuracy. Shame on the god if this is not the case.

The Bible is meaningless if the god did not direct the original and translated versions. If he did not, there is no way to know what is the word of the god and what is the word of a poet. We would be left on our own to pick and choose those parts that we think are true and to ignore the balance. We must apply the same logic to the argument that some parts are essential to its meaning and some parts are not essential. If any part is not essential, we must question why it is included at all. We should not need to get involved in these types of questions because there is no way that we can evaluate the validity of any answer to any of them. The god had, and if he exists, he still has, the ability to remove all doubt related to the accuracy of scripture.

The questions of inspiration and accurate translation of the Bible are compounded by its elasticity. It is clear that we are asked to take the word of a prisoner that a god inspired the Bible, and we can only hope that it was translated accurately, and that the twists and stretches of our particular priest are the truth. We must additionally concede that our own reasoning power is like a whore when we attempt to reconcile it with biblical teachings.

EVALUATING SCRIPTURE

We know that man's mind has the ability to acquire data and to integrate it with prior data. It is able to know what is true when it does that. If contradictions occur in this process, the mind must attempt to determine what is true and what is false. If it is diligent in this process, it will become more efficient and more accurate at determining what is true and what is false when required to make such determinations in the future. We know that all men whose minds are not limited in some way are capable of determining what is true and what is false in most situations if they are willing to do the mental work that is necessary for that task. The majority of men are perfectly able to evaluate the credibility of the Bible.

We are going to critique certain parts of the Bible. We are going to take the word of Paul that at least the Old Testament was inspired by this god. We must assume that the god did, and still does, have the ability to guarantee the accuracy of it. We are going to notice numerous discrepancies of various types. Each individual discrepancy raises the probability that all of scripture is a myth except to the minds that know square pegs will fit into round holes if we can just learn the secret. As discrepancies pile on top of discrepancies, perhaps some of those minds will begin to see the truth. Those that do will finally be free from the net of the priest.

We must acknowledge at this point that many Christians and some religions hold that you can't take the entire Bible literally. They tell us that we must read between the lines for its meaning. But since it is soft wax that can be molded and twisted to make it mean anything that one wants it to mean, whose interpretation of its meaning are we to use? Which priest do we want to consult to read between the lines for us and tell us what it all means? We must face a very basic fact in this regard. If we can't take it literally, it is of no value beyond that of any other collection of myths and fables.

PART III

Adventures and Fairy Tales

All quotations in this section will be taken from Genesis. We will be examining the creation and the flood. Quotes will be numbered and indented, but not in quotation marks.

Chapter I

1. In the beginning God created the heaven and the Earth

3. And God said, Let there be light: and there was light.

We note that the earth was created and it was illuminated in the absence of the sun, which was not as yet created.

4. ...and God divided the light from the darkness.

5. And God called the light Day, and the darkness he called Night. And the evening and the morning were the first day.

It's apparent that darkness existed prior to God's command for the creation of light. In order to take this verse seriously then, we must conclude that light and darkness existed together in the same place and time after the light was created. There was no need for God to divide them if this wasn't the case.

We learn in mid-school science that darkness is simply the absence of light. We learn also that the light that shines on earth comes from the sun, and that the darkness is caused by the shadow of the earth on the side of it that doesn't face the sun. But in order for God to have darkness and light on the first day so that it could be called a day, he somehow made it that way in the absence of the sun because the sun wasn't created until the fourth day. So verse 4 would have us believe that light is magically separated from darkness, and that the earth began to experience day and night without the benefit of the sun.

We also know that the earth revolves around the sun. So in order for the earth to exist as we know it, the sun would of necessity have to be created before the earth. There is unanimous agreement among scientists that the sun did exist first, and that the earth and the other planets originated from the sun. We must conclude that the biblical account is wrong.

> 6. And God said, "Let there be a firmament in the midst of the waters: and let it divide the waters from the waters."

> 7. And God made the firmament; and divided the waters which were under the firmament from the waters which were above the firmament: and it was so.

> 8. And God called the firmament Heaven: and the evening and the morning were the second day.

In this apparent effort to explain the source of rainwater, the waters were divided from the waters by a firmament. What exactly is a firmament? The god called it heaven. The dictionary calls it the vault or arch of the sky; the heavens. It sounds like something that is firm, but it really isn't firm. Maybe it's firm when it holds the water up, and not so firm when it lets the water fall. We know in any case that there is no real separation of the water in the sky from the water on land. The water that falls from the sky is the result of condensation of water vapor that is continually rising from the water on the land. There is nothing that separates them.

> 9. And God said, Let the waters under the heaven be gathered together unto one place, and let the dry land appear: and it was so.

> 10. And God called the dry land Earth; and the gathering together of the waters called he Seas.

Perhaps this explanation can be accepted in a very broad sense. The fact is that water seeks its own level due to the force of gravity. In order for the land to be separated from the waters, the god needed to either raise some portions of land to create higher elevations, or he needed to lower some portions of land in order to create valleys to hold the water.

> 11. And God said, Let the earth bring forth grass, the herb yielding seed, and the fruit-tree yielding fruit after his kind, whose seed is in itself, upon the earth: and it was so.

> 12. And the earth brought forth grass, and herb yielding seed after his kind, and the tree yielding fruit, whose seed was in itself, after his kind: and God saw that it was good.

The difficulty here is that grass and other plants cannot live, let alone grow and produce seed, without sunlight. The sun was not as yet created. Is this just another routine miracle, or is it another contradiction of fact?

For the benefit of those people who question the possibility that a god created the earth in six days, the priest tells us that one day in the life of the god could be equal to eternity for man. The 12th verse becomes even more problematic if that is the case. The earth could not possibly "bring forth grass, the herb yielding seed, and the fruit tree yielding fruit" for eternity without the sun that does not yet exist.

> 14. And God said, Let there be lights in the firmament of the heaven, to divide the day from the night; and let them be for signs, and for seasons, and for days, and years.

We will recall that the firmament that these lights are supposedly placed in separates the waters of the earth from those above the heavens. The 14th verse places the lights in the firmament, and the firmament is between the earth and the waters of heaven. This means that the sun is closer to the earth than the clouds that hold the rain-water. The earth might get a little toasty if that was the case. Verses 15 through 17 place all of the lights, including the stars, in the firmament.

That would mean that the stars are closer to the earth than the clouds are.

> 26. And God said, Let us make man in our image, after our likeness: and let them have dominion over the fish of the sea, and over the fowl of the air, and over the cattle, and over all the earth, and over every creeping thing that creepeth upon the earth.

> 27. So God created man in his own image, in the image of God created he him; male and female created he them.

We have been instructed that Adam was the first man and that Eve, almost an afterthought, was the first woman. Perhaps it's just a minor chronological error, but we note that Eve was not created until chapter II, verse 22.

> 28. And God blessed them, and God said unto them, Be fruitful, and multiply, and replenish the earth, and subdue it: and have dominion over the fish of the sea, and over the fowl of the air, and over every living thing that moveth upon the earth.

Man is one of nature's most poorly equipped animals in terms of his natural ability to compete with other animals for food and his own safety. Man's capacity for dominion over the earth is entirely within the reasoning power of his brain. We know that later in this episode that man will eat of the tree of knowledge, but as that is defined, it is limited to the knowledge of good and evil. Therefore we must assume that as of the 28th verse he was able to use his reasoning power.

The question that arises is, if man had never eaten of the tree of knowledge of good and evil, would he have been free to go about his business of being fruitful, multiplying and replenishing the earth without any repercussions from the god? Was it to be an "anything goes" situation if he had not eaten the forbidden fruit? That is with certainty the way that it appears. That doesn't mean that he wouldn't do evil things. It just means that he wouldn't know the difference. It also means that he wouldn't be able to communicate the difference to his children and his associates. The concept of rule by ideas rather than by force could not have come into being, because such rules are based upon value judgments of good and evil. Civilizations could have never developed under such conditions. Man would have been a rational wild animal. Are we to suppose that was what the god intended, or did the god *know* that the man he created couldn't resist temptation? Neither alternative sheds a positive light on his creation.

Chapter II

15. And the Lord God took the man, and put him into the garden of Eden, to dress it, and to keep it.

16. And the Lord God commanded the man, Saying, Of every tree of the garden thou mayest freely eat:

17. But of the tree of the knowledge of good and evil, thou shalt not eat of it: for in the day that thou eatest thereof thou shalt surely die.

We should note that the god lied to Adam when he said, "thou shalt surely die." We couldn't ask for a more positive statement, but Adam didn't die as promised. What are we to make of the god's promises if his very first one is broken?

The tone of the Bible is also established here. Fear is the first motivator, and it is one of two major themes throughout. Threats are handed down to man in the same manner as a parent seeking nothing less than strict obedience. Unquestioning obedience is all that is asked of man. In the absence of unquestioning obedience, we can expect nothing but harsh punishment from this god. The second theme is introduced shortly: that of guilt.

20. ...but for Adam there was not found an help meet for him.

21. And the Lord God caused a deep sleep to fall upon Adam, and he slept; and he took one of his ribs, and closed up the flesh instead thereof:

22. And the rib, which the Lord God had taken from man, made he a woman, and brought her unto the man.

In verse 27 of chapter I we learned, "man and woman created he them". Admitting that chronology is perhaps only a minor problem, let's assume that the god initially did forget to create woman, and that Eve was indeed created from Adam's rib as an afterthought. Was Adam created with genitalia? If so, we must wonder why. If not, was he put into another deep sleep so this minor addition could be made? At any rate, our omniscient god appears to be a little disorganized at this point. That seems odd when we consider the intricacy and precision of that which is referred to as creation, not to mention the wonder of the human mind.

23. And Adam said, This is now bone of my bones, and flesh of my flesh: she shall be called Woman, because she was taken out of man.

24. Therefore shall a man leave his father and his mother, and shall cleave unto his wife: and they shall be one flesh.

This is a most remarkable speech for the world's first human. Aside from the fact that this use of vocabulary couldn't have come from the first human, he also has insight into the future of family relationships. How is this possible? He has no knowledge of parents, and the concept of marriage seems more than a little advanced for this time in history. He had no parents to leave, and as yet he has no children to leave him. His help meet was just presented to him. He doesn't even know what she is yet. His statement is filled with complex concepts, each of which requires a chain of other simple and complex concepts before he could arrive at those he spoke of. We must conclude that the poet who wrote this story invented Adam after the basic family structure was already in place.

25. And they were both naked, the man and his wife, and were not ashamed.

That shouldn't be newsworthy with or without the knowledge of good and evil unless we believe that nakedness is intrinsically evil. We are soon to be so instructed.

If nakedness is intrinsically evil as scripture suggests, then it is true that the god, being omniscient chose to create man naked, and he therefore created man evil by that nakedness. In fact, if man is evil or even has a tendency toward evilness, that is the doing of the god, the same god who allegedly created man in his own image. Man is what he is either by an accident of nature, or by the creation of a god. If the latter is the case, the god is responsible for whatever man is.

Chapter III

1. Now the serpent was more subtle than any beast of the field which the Lord God had made: and he said unto the woman, Yea, hath God said, Ye shall not eat of every tree of the garden?

2. And the woman said unto the serpent, We may eat of the fruit of the trees of the garden.

3. But of the fruit of the tree which is in the midst of the garden, God hath said, Ye shall not eat of it, neither shall ye touch it, lest ye die.

4. And the serpent said unto the woman, Ye shall not surely die;

5. For God doth know, that in the day ye eat thereof, then your eyes shall be opened; and ye shall be as gods, knowing good and evil.

Now we have animals that discourse with humans concerning whether the god was serious about the penalty for eating of the forbidden fruit. This serpent with a brain smaller than a baby pea is conducting an intellectual discussion that goes beyond the capabilities of a young human. It also lacks the tongue, lips and larynx, which are essential for speech.

"and ye shall be as gods, knowing good and evil" instructs us that eating of the forbidden fruit will allow man to magically distinguish between good and evil. It assumes that good and evil exist in a vacuum: that they exist and can be recognized independent of actions, context or consequences, and that Adam and Eve would both possess this ability when they ate the forbidden fruit. This was allegedly the case when after eating the fruit they became aware of their nakedness and were ashamed.

But good and evil do not exist in a vacuum. They are not entities of their own. They are rational evaluations of the consequences of the actions taken by rational beings. We do not consider the killing of a deer by a puma to be evil. It is tragic for the deer, but the action of the puma is not evil. We would make a similar judgment if the puma killed a human: tragic but not evil. It is not until a human kills a human that we consider it to be evil. Good and evil then are defined by a rational evaluation of the consequences of specific actions that are carried out by human beings. We make value judgments of human actions based upon their known consequences. Those actions that are harmful to the things that we value are defined as evil. Those actions that are helpful to the things that we value are defined as good. So the proposition that "ye shall be as gods, knowing good and evil" is fallacious because value judgments require a value system upon which judgments can be made. The first humans, allegedly Adam and Eve, could not have developed a value system at this point in their existence.

We also know that different cultures and sub-cultures have different views about what is good and what is evil. If man was innately vested with the knowledge of good and evil, these cultural differences would not exist because there would be a universal agreement on this subject. It is likewise true that children would be vested with such knowledge. They would not require continuous training and coaching regarding this matter. It is obvious then that man did not magically acquire the knowledge of good and evil by eating of some forbidden fruit. He has instead over the course of time literally invented a system that defines good and evil that is based upon the ideals that he has come to "value".

It is reasonably safe to assert that the concept of good in any situation cannot exist prior to the concept of evil. If we lived in a perfect, sin free world, neither concept would exist. Man would just go about the business of living free of either of these judgments because there would be no negative actions and negative consequences to judge. It is not until the first murder occurs that we can make the judgment that murder is undesirable. We likewise cannot make the judgment that non-murder is desirable.

We can argue that when Cain killed Abel as a result of circumstances that were contrived by the god that he essentially didn't know what he was doing. A man had never killed another man before that time. Although the entire episode is an invention, a more reasonable scenario would find Cain and his family taken aback by the fact that Abel was dead since no human had died up to this point. They might perhaps arrive at some joint understanding that they didn't want their fellow humans to die, and that from that time forth one man was not to kill another man. One thing is certain; at the time of the murder, there could not have been a concept of murder or a value system that defined it. Another certainty is that second generation humans, Cain and Abel, did not till the ground and they did not keep sheep. They were scavengers.

The serpent's logic was actually superior to that of the god. If eating of the tree of knowledge would enable man to know good and evil, of what value would that knowledge be if at the same time man were to die as the god promised?

> 6. And when the woman saw that the tree was good for food, and that it was pleasant to the eyes, and a tree to be desired to make one wise; she took of the fruit thereof, and did eat it; and gave also unto her husband with her, and he did eat.

7. And the eyes of them both were opened, and they knew that they were naked: and they sewed fig-leaves together, and made themselves aprons.

This couple deserves a lot of credit for invention. They conceptualized the first aprons and figured out how to make them. That was no small feat. Without the benefit of a department store or a bazaar, they created (instantly it appears) a sewing device (some kind of needle and thread) from nothing but the raw materials available in the garden. The device must have been rather delicate too because fig leaves are not the strongest material with which to work. That was a pretty nice effort for the world's first humans.

There can be no concept of good in the absence of the concept of evil as we have previously observed. We must accept then that the good and evil aspects of man are both the creation of the god because the god created man just as he is. If the creation of the universe and man is the work of the god, it's reasonable to assume that the god had the ability to create man without sin. Even if the god only allowed for a tendency for sin, that would be a set-up for which there can be no justification. If we take the position that the god created the earth and man as a testing ground for man, we must conclude that the game was rigged from the beginning.

There are immutable laws that govern the nature of man just as there are laws that define the nature of a triangle. Only an idiot would expect a triangle to function like a wheel. Only a tyrant would create man as he is and then expect him to behave like something that he isn't. If the god created man, and he doesn't meet the god's expectations, then shame on the god. Man is man. We can love him, pity him or hate him, but we can't make him into something other than man.

Chapter IV

1. And Adam knew Eve his wife; and she conceived, and bare Cain, and said, I have gotten a man from the Lord.

2. And she again bare his brother Abel. And Abel was a keeper of sheep, but Cain was a tiller of the ground.

3. And in process of time it came to pass, that Cain brought of the fruit of the ground an offering unto the Lord.

4. And Abel, he also brought of the firstlings of his flock and of the fat thereof. And the Lord had respect unto Abel, and to his offering:

5. But unto Cain, and to his offering, he had not respect: and Cain was very wroth, and his countenance fell.

As we observed earlier, second generation humans were neither tillers of the ground nor keepers of sheep. But we must examine what allegedly happened here. Abel was a keeper of sheep, but Cain was a mere tiller of the ground. Had there actually been a division of labor at that time, one of the men would have to have one specialty, and of necessity the other would have to have a different specialty. And it might be that a god, but more probably a priest, would prefer the sweet taste of a fat young sheep to the bland taste of a potato or a turnip. Cain's offering was the particular fruit of his labor just as was that of Abel. The fact that his offering wasn't as desirable as Abel's does not justify the god's reaction to it. Had their specialties been reversed, the god would have had no respect for the offering of Abel. If this absurd set-up were repeated today, we can be sure that the offering of the goldsmith would meet with favor, but woe unto the one that offers a box of apples.

But this ridiculous episode deserves our particular interest and examination for reasons that overshadow its absurdity. Cain and Abel each made an "offering" unto the Lord. Most of us have been brainwashed since our infancy with the notion that we have a moral obligation to sacrifice part of our wealth to this god. We don't even question the actions of Cain and Abel. But shouldn't we do so? Certainly this omniscient, omnipotent god didn't need these offerings. After all, he is the alleged source of everything on the planet. He has not requested any sacrifices up to this point in scripture. It seems that Cain came up with this notion out of the blue, and that Abel just followed his brother's lead.

If we consider the simple facts of this situation, must we not conclude that both the fruit of the ground and the fatted lamb would rot in the sun and be wasted? Can we believe that this is what this god desired? Of course we can't. But when we stop to remember that priests and their agents wrote the Bible, the episode takes on its true nature. The priest does require food, and he receives it under the guise of a gift to the god. This little episode sets the stage for sacrifices to this god, and the priests repeat and refine it throughout scripture until at last man is to sacrifice himself to everybody that can attach the word "needy" to themselves.

Chapter VI

5. And God saw that the wickedness of man was great in the earth, and that every imagination of the thoughts of his heart was only evil continually.

You, Dear Reader, are part of the family of man. Do you really believe that this verse is a true depiction of you? Do you believe that it is a true depiction of the members of your family? Do you believe that it is a true depiction of most of the people that you know?

6. And it repented the Lord that he had made man on the earth, and it grieved him at his heart.

7. And the Lord said, I will destroy man whom I have created from the face of the earth; both man, and beast, and the creeping thing, and the fowls of the air; for it repenteth me that I have made them.

8. But Noah found grace in the eyes of the Lord.

The previous four verses contain the crux of both the Old Testament and the New Testament. Herein lies the essence of the entire

Christian myth; a myth designed to enslave men by their guilt, their fear and their hope. They are taught that they are low, unworthy creatures. They are taught to fear the wrath of the god. They are taught to pray for forgiveness and to hope for salvation. Freedom from all of this lies in simply understanding what takes place in these four verses.

This god created heaven and earth and all that exists in them. He created the universe and life itself; more forms of both plant and animal life than the average man will likely experience in a lifetime. He created the human brain, a brain capable of cognition, and capable of storing, cataloging and evaluating that which it is cognizant of, and it frequently does all of these things instantly and simultaneously. This god is omnipotent. He is also omniscient because we are told that he is observing and judging every thought and act of every living person. That amounts to some six billion people at the time of this writing. This is surely a god capable of knowing and doing anything.

We must ask then how such a wonderful and powerful god could possibly in one instance be either stupid or naive. He observed that every imagination of the thoughts of man's heart was evil continually. Yet Noah found grace in the eyes of the god. Therefore Noah and his sons and their respective wives were saved from destruction. The fact that Noah was a good and just man, and that he found grace in the eyes of the god, doesn't change the fundamental fact the he and his sons suffered from the same design flaw as all other men did. The thing, whatever it was, that made man evil, was still a part of man's nature. Whatever it was about man that had been so troublesome to this god was still there. Being the omniscient being that he was, the god had to know it. And knowing it he could have, and logically would have, stuck to his original idea of destroying the whole messy project. Saving Noah and his sons from the destruction was absurd, just as absurd as the crucifixion of Jesus was to save man from eternal damnation.

The entire Christian myth comes down to these few essentials. A god created the universe and man. The god created man with a troublesome flaw. The god recognized the flaw and decided to destroy his creation. But he liked one of the men and decided to spare him and his sons from the destruction even though they had the flaw themselves. As a result, man's behavior continued to be problematic to the god. Somehow the god decided that man should have eternal life, but he couldn't permit such a thing to such an evil being. Knowing that man couldn't change his own nature, the god decided to have a son whom he would offer up unto himself as a sacrifice and atonement for the flawed nature that he had created in man.

It's impossible to imagine a more absurd scenario than the preceding one, but that is precisely what the creation, the flood and the crucifixion of Jesus amounts to. This is not the work of an omniscient, omnipotent god. This is the work of men: men who want to control the minds and the purse strings of their fellows.

Luther had an interesting, and essentially self-contradictory take on the crucifixion. He "rejected with horror the notion that in the Mass the priest offers up Christ to His Father as a sacrifice in atonement for man's sins—though he found nothing horrible in the idea that God had allowed man to crucify God as a sacrifice to God in atonement for man's sins."(1) Most of us would find both scenarios horrible as well as absurd.

We continue with this fairy tale.

> 15. And this is the fashion which thou shalt make it of: The length of the ark shall be three hundred cubits, the breadth of it fifty cubits, and the height of it thirty cubits.

This was to be a magnificent ship. We learn a little later that the waters raised upward fifteen cubits and covered the mountains. Mount Ararat, where the arc allegedly settled, is 16,946 feet high. Now if fifteen cubits of water covered the mountains, a cubit has to be slightly more than 1000 feet in order for the water to cover Mount Ararat. The arc then was 32,000 feet tall: twice as tall as Mount Ararat. It was 320,000 feet long: about sixty-one miles long, and 53,000 feet wide: ten miles wide. How can we possibly believe this? We can't of course.

We can take a more conservative approach and use the table of measures provided by our Bible source wherein it is stated that a cubit is equal to 1.824 feet. This puts the height at 54.72 feet, the length at 547.2 feet and the width at 91.2 feet. Oh yes! This is much more believable. This ship is slightly less than two football fields long, about the width of the distance between the bases of a baseball diamond and slightly taller than a five story building. This ship would only require the harvesting, cutting and transporting of a few thousand trees, and a few hundred thousand hours to assemble. Noah and his boys could easily throw this little thing together in the evenings after they attended to the normal business of existence. We must suppose that their evil neighbors were not aware of this little boat because there is no mention that they had to be restrained from forcing their way on board when the big rain started.

Chapter VII

12. And the rain was upon the earth forty days and forty nights.

20. Fifteen cubits upward did the waters prevail; and the mountains were covered.

Chapter VIII

1. And God remembered Noah, and every living thing, and all the cattle that was with him in the ark: and God made a wind to pass over the earth, and the waters assuaged;

2. The fountains also of the deep, and the windows of heaven were stopped, and the rain from heaven was restrained;

3. And the waters returned from off the earth continually: and after the end of the hundred and fifty days the waters were abated.

4. And the ark rested in the seventh month, on the seventeenth day of the month, upon the mountains of Ararat.

The flood raises many other questions that cannot be reconciled with fact and reason. We will point out just a few. Those of blind faith can explain them away by the miraculous powers of the god. Those who truly seek the truth can add them to the evidence that scripture is a myth.

We can begin with the fact that there is not enough water on the earth to cover even the foothills, let alone the peak of Ararat or any other mountain ranges. If the last drop of moisture fell from the sky, and all of the glaciers and ice caps were melted, only the very lowest portions of the earth would be flooded.

If the earth had been covered with water to the extent described in Genesis, it would require over fourteen years for all of it to evaporate. This assumes that it was heated to 212 degrees and that it all remained in the atmosphere after it evaporated. At normal temperatures, it would never subside because as it evaporated the moisture would condense in the atmosphere and create more rain. The earth would continually be immersed in water.

Supposing that the flood came and left as described in scripture, the soil of the earth would be totally saturated after 150 days. Much of the plant life that we have today could not have survived that length of time under water.

It's commendable that the carnivores aboard the arc restrained themselves from devouring their natural source of life for 150 days. What happened after they left the arc? There were only two each of their natural prey. Did the carnivores hibernate until the rabbits, deer and elk had reproduced enough to insure that there would be an adequate meat supply from then until eternity? That would take several years. We would have had a lot of very lean carnivores by then.

The oceans would have lost virtually all of their salinity during the flood. How did the fish that require salt water survive in a fresh water environment for 150 days?

Chapter IX

12. And God said, This is the token of the covenant which I make between me and you and every living creature that is with you, for perpetual generations.

13. I do set my bow in the cloud, and it shall be for a token of a covenant between me and the earth.

14. And it shall come to pass, when I bring a cloud over the earth, that the bow shall be in the cloud.

15. And I will remember my covenant, which is between me and you and every living creature of all flesh; and the waters shall no more become a flood to destroy all flesh.

Although it isn't specifically stated in scripture that rainbows didn't exist prior to the flood, that is the implication of these verses. Science tells us that rainbows are the natural phenomenon of light rays of the sun being refracted by mist or drops of rain in the sky. If this is the case, rainbows existed prior to the flood, unless of course, the god's unnatural, supernatural powers somehow prevented such refraction of light rays. If that was the case, he was performing a miracle in anticipation of the flood and of the covenant he would later make. Now if that was the case, the entire scenario had to have been planned from the beginning of creation.

Let's return to chapter VIII,

21. ...I will not again curse the ground any more for man's sake; for the imagination of man's heart is evil from his youth;...

It's curious that the god would choose to spare Noah and his family if this was his evaluation of man. It appears that he does indeed recognize that his experiment was a failure; that is, man is hopelessly evil. Noah and the ark appear to be nothing more than an extension of the game, a game that cannot be won by man, but must be a continuous harassment of man by a god that cannot be pleased. Better for the god and man that the ark had never been constructed. But then what would the god have done with his time for the rest of eternity?

The critical reader could go on indefinitely asking these kinds of questions, and there are only two possible answers to them. This god of scripture actually manipulated the lives of ancient man with miracles piled on top of miracles, or the entire account is false. Some will suggest that it isn't necessary to take all of these accounts literally. To that we must then ask, "Is it fact or is it fiction? If we can't determine one from the other, how can we believe any of it and of what value is it?"

PART IV

According to Luke

EVIL AND ANARCHY

The advent of Jesus and of Christianity introduced more than just a new perspective of man's relationship with the god. It introduced a totally new philosophy of life and a new view as to how man was to deal with his fellows. In this section we will again critique scripture to determine the authenticity of the story. Later we will examine the impact of the doctrine of Christianity itself. We will use the account of Luke to follow Jesus' tenure upon the earth because Luke is the only scribe who contends that his sources were eyewitnesses to the events, and that he had a perfect understanding of these things from the very beginning.

Chapter I

1. Foreasmuch as many have taken in hand to set forth in order a declaration of those things which are most surely believed among us,

2. Even as they delivered them unto us, which from the beginning were eye-witnesses, and ministers of the word;

3. It seemed good to me also, having had perfect understanding of all things from the very first, to write unto thee in order, most excellent Theophilus,

4. That thou mightest know the certainty of those things wherein thou hast been instructed.

It seems that eyewitnesses were essential to Luke in order for these tales to be convincing to the "most excellent Theophilus" whom must have been a person of authority and power; probably enough power to establish a religious belief within a city or region. After all, education wasn't wasted on the average herdsman or fisherman two thousand years ago, and the salutation "most excellent" indicates that he was a person of considerable importance. At any rate, Luke, having received this information from eyewitnesses, records the experiences of Jesus for Theophilus and for us based upon those witnesses rather than by divine inspiration.

Neither Luke nor his frequent companion, Saint Paul, knew Jesus while he lived. Luke and Paul both lived during the time that the disciples began preaching the gospel, and it is believed that Luke was one of the seventy disciples. It would seem that one or more of the apostles would necessarily be the eyewitnesses that he refers to. Our task then is to determine if any of the apostles could have been witnesses to the events described. We will also question the logic and reasoning of parts of the account. Let us begin.

> 13. But the angel said unto him, Fear not, Zacharias: for thy prayer is heard; and thy wife Elisabeth shall bear thee a son, and thou shalt call his name John.

Did one of the apostles witness that? Then who did?

> 28. And the angel came in unto her, and said, Hail, thou that art highly favoured, the Lord is with thee: Blessed art thou among women.

> 31. And, behold, thou shalt conceive in thy womb, and bring forth a son, and shalt call his name JESUS.

> 35. And the angel answered and said unto her, The Holy Ghost shall come upon thee, and the power of the Highest shall overshadow thee: therefore also that holy thing which shall be born of thee, shall be called the Son of God.

36. And behold, thy cousin Elisabeth, she hath also conceived a son in her old age; and this is the sixth month with her who was called barren:

39. And Mary arose in those days, and went into the hill country with haste, into a city of Juda,

40. And entered into the house of Zacharias, and saluted Elisabeth.

41. And it came to pass, that when Elisabeth heard the salutation of Mary, the babe leaped in her womb: and Elisabeth was filled with the Holy Ghost.

Who were the eyewitnesses to those events? The circumstances would indicate that there were no witnesses of any kind. How could any person have given this information to Luke?

Chapter II

25. And behold, there was a man in Jerusalem, whose name was Simeon: and the same man was just and devout, waiting for the consolation of Israel: and the Holy Ghost was upon him.

26. And it was revealed unto him by the Holy Ghost, that he should not see death, before he had seen the Lord's Christ.

27. And he came by the spirit into the temple; and when the parents brought in the child Jesus, to do for him after the custom of the law,

28. Then took he him up in his arms, and blessed God, and said,

29. Lord, now lettest thou thy servant depart in peace, according to thy word:

30. For mine eyes have seen thy salvation,

31. Which thou hast prepared before the face of all people;

32. A light to lighten the Gentiles, and the glory of thy people Israel.

33. And Joseph and his mother marvelled at those things which were spoken of him.

We can perhaps understand that Joseph would marvel. Perhaps Mary had failed to tell him that their son was actually the Son of God. But if that was the case, how did he suppose that she had conceived? Mary should not marvel on any account. Gabriel had told her what was to happen, and the Holy Ghost had come upon her. She knew that her son was the Son of God. Surely the god wouldn't choose an idiot girl to bear his child, and it would seem that indeed he didn't. If we go back to her chapter 1 meeting with Elisabeth she addresses the meaning of the birth of her child.

46. And Mary said, My soul doth magnify the Lord,

47. And my spirit hath rejoiced in God my Saviour.

48. For he hath regarded the low estate of his handmaiden: for behold, from henceforth all generations shall call me blessed.

49. For he that is mighty hath done to me great things; and holy is his name.

Mary was well aware of the nature of her child. There can be no reason for her to marvel at the words of Simeon. Logically there was no reason to keep the nature of the conception from Joseph. Indeed, we would think that she would have eagerly shared that information with him lest he suspect that the child was a bastard. Had she done the logical and supposedly honest thing, Joseph would not marvel at Simeon's words either.

Their amazement is equally curious in chapter 2 when they discovered that he was not with the company as they returned from the feast of the Passover during his twelfth year.

46. And it came to pass, that after three days they found him in the temple, sitting in the midst of the doctors, both hearing them, and asking them questions.

47. And all that heard him were astonished at his understanding and answers.

48. And when they saw him, they were amazed: and his mother said unto him, Son, why hast thou thus dealt with us? behold, thy father and I have sought thee sorrowing.

49. And he said unto them, How is it that ye sought me? wist ye not that I must be about my Father's business?

50. And they understood not the saying which he spake unto them.

The same question about witnesses is pertinent to both of these temple experiences. And why wouldn't Mary, at least, understand the meaning of his statement?

Chapter III

3. And he (John the Baptist) came into all the country about Jordan, preaching the baptism of repentance, for the remission of sins;

This is the introduction of atonement; man's new relationship with his god and with his fellows. We see it in various forms in the New Testament. Atonement is based upon the proposition that man is evil by nature and incapable of attaining the god's grace on his own merit. Faith and repentance are the new tickets to personal salvation. The entire concept of atonement and the remission of sins amount to the sacrifice of the just man to the unjust man, and we will explore this development in some detail later in this section.

9. And now also the axe is laid unto the root of the trees: every tree therefore which bringeth not forth good fruit, is hewn down, and cast into the fire.

10. And the people asked him, saying, What shall we do then?

11. He answereth and saith unto them, He that hath two coats, let him impart to him that hath none; and he that hath meat, let him do likewise.

This is the beginning of the altruist code. It is repeated in various forms throughout the New Testament. We will challenge the morality of altruism in some detail later.

Verses 24 through 38 of chapter three gives a theoretic chronology of Jesus' ancestry back to the creation. We know that there is no written history that goes back to the alleged creation, and it is preposterous to assume that Jewish genealogy could be traced back that far. So we must have a very elastic imagination to buy into Luke's account. But if we are willing to take Luke's genealogy at face value, we still have a couple of small problems here.

The first deals with the timing of the creation from a scriptural perspective as opposed to how old the earth is. Our biblical source states that the time elapsed between the creation of the earth and the birth of Jesus was 3974 years, six months and ten days. Now this is a very precise account, and very interesting when we consider that early man had not yet learned how to measure time, and he didn't know how to write. Therefore neither the time account nor the genealogy account has any credence. Science puts the age of the earth at millions of years, not at several thousand years.

The genealogical account is actually pointless also. It's a history of Joseph's ancestry, not Jesus'. Since Mary was allegedly a virgin and Joseph was not the father of Jesus, it makes absolutely no sense to validate Joseph's ancestry. It would make more sense to give an account of Mary's ancestry if it were important to know about Jesus' bloodline.

Chapter IV

The early verses of this chapter deal with the temptations by Satan. We will make two points about the temptations without quoting scripture. First, it's absurd to think that the alleged son of the god could be tempted with anything. He is the chosen one of the supposed almighty. He is virtually on a par with the creator of all of the stuff that Satan is attempting to tempt him with, and he knows who he is. Why "the Spirit" led him into the wilderness for forty days is as mysterious as why Satan thought he could tempt him. The entire episode is preposterous. The second point is that there could have been no witnesses to communicate these particular events.

> *18.* The Spirit of the Lord is upon me, because he hath anointed me to preach the gospel to the poor;

We must ask why the Lord would single out the poor to hear the gospel.

> 41. And devils also came out of many, crying out, and saying, Thou art Christ the Son of God. And he rebuking them, suffered them not to speak: for they knew that he was Christ.

These little devils had been cast out of those with "divers diseases". Do we believe that devils are the cause of disease? Were they the cause of disease two thousand years ago? Do devils talk to mortals when they enter or exit their bodies? Why would Jesus "suffer them not to speak"? Some people do believe in devils and some actually talk to them just as some believe in witches and their craft. Like Luther, many people are taught this stuff by their parents. "Both parents believed in witches, elves, angels, and demons of many kinds and specialties; and Martin (Luther) carried most of these superstitions with him to the end. A religion of terror in a home of rigorous discipline...."(1) The vast majority of men have never seen, heard or talked to a witch, elf, angel or any kind of demon. Why is that so? What must we think of those who did? What do we think of those who do now?

Chapter VI

24. But woe unto you that are rich! For ye have received your consolation.

25. Woe unto you that are full! For ye shall hunger. Woe unto you that laugh now! For ye shall mourn and weep.

26. Woe unto you, when all men shall speak well of you! For so did their fathers to the false prophets.

27. But I say unto you which hear, Love your enemies, do good to them which hate you,

28. Bless them that curse you, and pray for them which despitefully use you.

29. And unto him that smiteth thee on the one cheek, offer also the other; and him that taketh away thy cloak, forbid not to take thy coat also.

30. Give to every man that asketh of thee; and of him that taketh away thy goods, ask them not again.

31. And as ye would that men should do to you, do ye also to them likewise.

32. For if ye love them which love you, what thank have ye? for sinners also love those that love them.

33. And if ye do good to them which do good to you, what thank have ye? for sinners also do even the same.

34. And if ye lend to them of whom ye hope to receive, what thank have ye? for sinners also lend to sinners, to receive as much again.

35. But love ye your enemies, and do good, and lend, hoping for nothing again; and your reward shall be great, and ye shall be the children of the Highest: for he is kind unto the unthankful and to the evil.

36. Be ye therefore merciful, as your Father also is merciful.

37. Judge not, and ye shall not be judged: condemn not, and ye shall not be condemned: forgive, and ye shall be forgiven:

These verses pretty well summarize the teachings of Jesus. We know that nobody really believes that man can live by this code. This is the code of submission to everything that we despise. It is enslavement of those that would follow it by all men who would not follow it, and it is the code of enslavement via personal guilt to the priest. This is a code of total anarchy. Let's review.

The rich are condemned. Now who is to determine who is rich? To the penniless beggar, virtually every other person is too rich. To the average worker, his employer is too rich. To the mediocre business-man, the very successful businessman is too rich. Does this mean woe to those who have any more wealth than anybody else has? Does this mean that we should reduce all wealth to the lowest common denominator? And if we were inclined to do so, and could find a way to do so, how are we to maintain that status? Nobody, not even the penniless beggar desires such an outcome. Does this mean that wealth, man's vehicle to survival, is categorically evil? If not, what does it mean?

"Woe unto you that laugh now." Is laughter evil? Is man not to experience joy and mirth?

"Woe unto you, when all men shall speak well of you!" Does this mean woe to those who are praised for being helpful, friendly, courte-ous, kind, obedient, cheerful, thrifty, brave, clean and reverent? Is it better that we are cursed for being the opposite? Or does it just mean woe to those who are praised for anything? Are we to be cursed for any sign of personal pride?

"Love your enemies, do good to them which hate you." Does this mean that we should assist those who would destroy us?

Bless them that curse you, turn the other cheek, don't challenge the thief, and give whatever is asked of you. In other words, we are to treat our personal existence as though it is of lesser value than that of those who harm us or intend to harm us. We are to condone and support evil whenever it is directed at us.

"For if ye love them which love you, what thank have ye? For sinners also love those that love them." Doesn't this denigrate the entire meaning of love? Are we to tell our loved ones that we don't love them because they are wonderful, but because they are miserable, and that they make us miserable? Are we to love them because we know that they don't love us? Are we to tell them that we forsook a relationship with somebody that we absolutely adored in order that we could be with somebody that we abhor? Is the meaning of love to be inverted in order to follow these ravings?

"and ye shall be the children of the Highest: for he is kind unto the unthankful and to the evil." This is an interesting twist. Evil is to be rewarded for being evil.

The moral fundamentals of the new belief system: atonement/forgiveness, non-judgment and altruism are now in place. The teachings of John and Jesus replaced the Law of Moses. Man's relationship with the god and with other men was altered. Civilization made a wrong turn, and we will address the magnitude of this change after we examine a little more of Luke's story.

Chapter VIII

38. Now, the man out of whom the devils were departed, besought him that he might be with him. But Jesus sent him away, saying,

39. Return to thine own house, and shew how great things God hath done unto thee. And he went his way and published throughout the whole city, how great things Jesus had done unto him.

55. And her spirit came again, and she arose straightway: and he commanded to give her meat.

56. And her parents were astonished: but he charged them that they should tell no man what was done.

Can there be any logical reason for Jesus to want his miracles published in the first case but kept secret in the second case? No. But then what does logic have to do with scripture?

Chapter XII

In part one of this book we discussed the division that religion has created among men, and the fact that there is a contradiction in Luke's account. We should not casually accept it or overlook it. Luke tells us in chapter II, verses 13 and 14:

> And suddenly there was with the angel a multitude of the heavenly host praising God, and saying, Glory to God in the highest, and on earth peace, good will toward men.
>   Now in Chapter XII, verse 51 Luke tells us:
>   Suppose ye that I am come to give peace on earth? I tell you, Nay; but rather division.

We have previously noted that religion including Christianity has brought division rather than peace on earth. But shouldn't it give us some pause that the contradiction exists at all. The first statement came from a multitude of the heavenly host. Must we not assume that the heavenly host were messengers of the god? As such, we must believe that they were aware of the god's purpose, and that purpose was stated to be peace on earth, and good will toward men. But now in chapter XII, Jesus states the opposite. How is it that the heavenly host of the god and the son of the god are in total disagreement over this fundamental position? How could an omnipotent god allow his heavenly host to make one statement to the shepherds, and to have his son make a contradictory statement?

We must question Luke as well as the god. Luke was a man of letters and certainly not an idiot. Wouldn't he who was writing to the most excellent Theophilus question this major contradiction himself? He was after all writing to one whom was probably a powerful and knowledgeable man. It would behoove him to either explain the contradiction or to question his sources. Certainly he would have questioned it himself. Well, maybe he wouldn't after all. Maybe he was just another poet trying to sell a story. Maybe he didn't write all of it. Maybe he didn't write any of it. Maybe he didn't see a contradiction. What should we think?

Chapter XVI

32. And he said unto them, Ye are they which justify yourselves before men; but God knoweth your hearts: for that which is highly esteemed among men is abomination in the sight of God.

Why is this so? Is there nothing that man can value that can please this god? Apparently not. This god hates man's source of survival, mutual respect, mutual admiration and even life itself.

Chapter XVIII

14. I tell you, this man went down to his house justified rather than the other: for every one that exalteth himself shall be abased; and he that humbleth himself shall be exalted.

A man shall take no credit for his accomplishments. He must instead demean himself, and if he has success at anything, he must give the credit to this god. We see this humility most frequently among athletes. Why is it that a man or woman who has devoted virtually all of their time and energy in order to excel in some endeavor should give the credit for their achievement to this god? They set their goal. They drove themselves. They produced the results.

22. Now, when Jesus heard these things, he said unto him, Yet lackest thou one thing: sell all that thou hast, and distribute unto the poor, and thou shalt have treasure in heaven: and come, follow me.

This is all that is asked: give up all that you have and follow me. Everything in this life must be sacrificed in order to find that eternal life in heaven. What would our life be like if everybody actually did that? What would life be like if every single person gave all of their wealth to the poor and followed Jesus? What if nobody was out there producing food, clothing and shelter? It wouldn't be very long before all that had been produced was consumed. Everybody would be following Jesus, but there would be no food. Would all of us, including the priest, be able to rely upon the bounty of the god?

Chapter XXI

32. Verily, I say unto you, This generation shall not pass away, till all be fulfilled.

33. Heaven and earth shall pass away: but my words shall not pass away.

Did it happen that way? Here we are two thousand years later, and many, many generations have passed away, but the earth is still here. If Jesus didn't really mean "this generation", why didn't he say what he really meant? If he really didn't mean the "earth shall pass away", what did he mean?

Chapter XXII

47. And while he yet spake, behold a multitude, and he that was called Judas, one of the twelve, went before them, and drew near unto Jesus to kiss him.

48. But Jesus said unto him, Judas, betrayest thou the Son of man with a kiss?

49. When they which were about him saw what would follow, they said unto him, Lord, shall we smite with the sword?

50. And one of them smote the servant of the high priest, and cut off his right ear.

51. And Jesus answered and said, Suffer ye thus far. And he touched his ear, and healed him.

52. Then Jesus said unto the chief priests, and captains of the temple, and the elders which were come to him, Be ye come out as against a thief, with swords and staves?

53. When I was daily with you in the temple, ye stretched forth no hands against me: but this is your hour, and the power of darkness.

The story of the betrayal makes no sense other than it was necessary to fulfill an Old Testament prophecy. Essentially one book of adventures is used to validate the other book of adventures, but the betrayal wasn't necessary in order for the priests, captains and elders to identify Jesus. Jesus said as much in the fifty-second verse. Additionally his fame is attested to in IV-14, V-15, VIII-39, IXX-47, XX-19 and XXI-38. The betrayal wasn't necessary for the purpose of identifying Jesus. He was famous, and he personally knew those who wanted to take his life. If the betrayal wasn't necessary from the point of view of the priests, why would they pay Judas for doing it? Did they have a vested interest in the fulfillment of the prophecy? They absolutely did not. Add this to the list of absurd scenarios.

We must wonder whether Luke had some ulterior motive in his story of the discussion between Pilate and the chief priests. Three times Pilate found no fault with Jesus, but the priests prevailed upon him to crucify Jesus. So Pilate gives them their wish in spite of finding no fault. This would play well with the most excellent Theophilus and other Roman leaders because they are thus excused of any responsibility for Jesus' execution. They might well be influenced to give succor to Luke and the other disciples as they set out to convert the most powerful nation in the world to Christianity.

Chapter XXIV

6. He is not here, but is risen. Remember how he spake unto you when he was yet in Galilee,

7. Saying, The Son of man must be delivered into the hands of sinful men, and be crucified, and the third day rise again.

8. And they remembered his words,

9. And returned from the sepulchre, and told all these things unto the eleven, and to all the rest.

10. It was Mary Magdalene, and Joanna, and Mary the mother of James, and other women that were with them, which told these things unto the apostles.

11. And their words seemed to them as idle tales, and they believed them not.

It is indeed difficult to believe such a tale. The apostles, however, had allegedly been witnesses to so many miracles that were performed by this man. Surely they would not doubt that he was resurrected. If these first-hand witnesses who had seen him walk on water, feed hosts of people with seven fishes, heal the blind and the lepers, and resurrect the dead, could not believe that he was resurrected, who in the world could ever be expected to believe it? No rational man could be expected to believe it. No man that trusts his own mind, and his own logic really does believe it.

In spite of the multitude of unbelievable events that take place in the myths of scripture, Christian religions boast millions of followers. Those millions include many millions who are intelligent, educated and rational. How can we account for that?

There is no way to know what goes on within the minds of any one of them, but we can make some reasonable assumptions. We can suppose that these millions can be divided into two general classifications: the total believers and those who are not so sure. We cannot speculate as to the proportion that each of these groups make up of the total. We also know that within both groups, that there are huge majorities who have never read the Bible in its entirety. Of those who have, it is safe to assume that most did so without serious study.

As mentioned in our foreword, the total believers, the faithful, are not interested in logic. *Faith is free from the necessity of being logical.* Therefore, in spite of all of the irrationality of scripture, there can be no valid contradiction to faith. These people, whether large or small in number, accept scripture as true, period, no questions.

We will speculate that the not so sure group is larger than the totally faithful group. Most of them have not read the Bible, and like their counterparts, those who have read it did so in a very casual manner. Some have at times questioned the validity of these adventurous fairly tales, but it is not a serious issue for them. Some have never given a thought to the issue. Some perform the rituals of their particular religious denomination on a regular basis. Some go to church for Christmas and Easter services. Some never go to church, but are still counted as members of one church or another. Many, no doubt, live the guise of a believer because it is socially and politically expedient to do so. So we can see that though the numbers of people who are counted as Christians is large, the numbers that totally believe in the teachings of the Bible are in question.

Regardless of the number of believers, whether it is large or small, the only number that is important is one, the individual. The important question for each individual is whether he trusts his mind, his primary tool for survival, or will he negate his mind, the essence of man. If he negates his mind, he reduces man to a primal animal, an animal driven by instinct and fear. He returns to the primeval forest to be tortured by the demons that were conjured up by his prehistoric ancestors.

PART V

Philosophy for Chaos

While Christian teachings are about one's relationship with their god, they are also and more importantly about relationships with their fellow men. We need to examine the essence of the latter in order to determine if these teachings are valid as a way of relating to one another even though they did not originate from a god. We noted earlier that the behavioral cornerstones of Christian doctrine are non-judgment, forgiveness and altruism. We will examine those three in detail. The various other admonitions of Jesus that lead man on the course of self-destruction stand on their own as unworthy of consideration by a rational being.

NON-JUDGMENT

Do we need a reminder that the god saw that the wickedness of man was great in the earth, and that every imagination of the thoughts of his heart was only evil continually? If this is in fact the case, it seems that a negative judgment by man is in perfect agreement with that of the god. Are we not to agree with the god, or are we not to judge that some men are not as bad as all that? Are we not to make positive judgments as well as negative ones? Are we at fault regardless of how we judge another man?

It is not uncommon to hear someone say, "Who am I to judge", or to paraphrase Jesus with, "Let he who has not sinned cast the first stone." This might sound like a humble Christian acknowledging his own lack of perfection and therefore his justifiable unwillingness to pass judgment on someone else. Simply stated it says, "Nobody's perfect, therefore nobody should judge." Now if enough people believe this, and acknowledging their own imperfection, agree that no judgment should be made, a questionable act by one of our fellows is accepted without review or censure.

We can accept the fact that none of us is perfect. But should this prevent us from making judgments about those actions of our peers that we think might be wrong and harmful to us as individuals or to our group? The answer is that perfection, or lack of it, has nothing to do with the issue at hand. The issue is whether a member of our group has acted in a way that is harmful to the group or one of its members. If we are concerned about the well being of the group and the individuals that make it up, we must pass judgment. To do otherwise causes immediate and future risk of harm to each individual member of the group. Groups establish rules that are intended to ensure the safety and well being of its members. The willingness of the members of a group to pass judgment on the actions of other members is precisely what makes a group strong and membership in it valuable. So it should be apparent that non-judgment is not a valid option for any member of the group.

The truth of the matter is that judgment is precisely what makes personal and group relationships work. The fact that parents define for their children what actions are acceptable and what actions are not acceptable determines how their children behave. The same is true in the case of all relationships. If we value the relationship with our spouse, our parents, our neighbors and our co-workers, we will choose to behave in ways that we think will gain and maintain a good relationship with them. We behave in ways that we believe they will judge to be favorable. If we communicate to them what actions we appreciate, they will respond to us in a positive way if they value their relationship with us.

On the other hand, if nobody ever passed judgment on the actions of others, the entire world would be one of chaos: total, absolute chaos.

If we had no expectations of others, or if we failed to communicate our expectations, nobody would know how to behave around us, and we wouldn't know how to behave around others. All actions would be random actions. Under such circumstances we would all be doing whatever we wanted to do at any time and at any place that we wanted to do it. Of course the physically strong would dominate such a world just as they do in the world of our animal cousins.

Judgment is what activates that "base" human trait that we call "pride". How we want others to judge us helps to determine whether we mow the lawn, wash the windows, go to work or take a bath. Our personal pride in the totality of our existence is driven to a large extent by our judgment of ourselves and by the judgment of others. We see then that judgment is essential to civilization, and it is essentially what elevates man from his basic animal behavior.

Non-judgment is selfish. To choose non-judgment in order to avoid the judgment of a god is to put our personal well being in front of the well being of our society. This is selfishness at its most fundamental level. To choose non-judgment in order to avoid the censure or wrath of a family member, neighbor or co-worker is to be cowardly and selfish. To refuse to pass judgment upon the wrongful actions of others is to condone evil by default. Judgment is essential to relationships and to civilization. If there were such a thing as an omniscient god, it would not ask its "children" to condone every sort of evil by abstaining from judgment.

We delegate the role of judgment to juries and judges within our legal system. It is not a stretch of the imagination to believe that most of these people are Christians and that when it comes to the punishment phase of the law, many of these people are swayed by the Christian doctrine of non-judgment and its accomplice, leniency. Perhaps caught up in their own sense of non-perfection, judges and jurors mistakenly believe therefore that they have a humane responsibility to be lenient with the criminal. It should be obvious that this is not the case, and it should be equally obvious that they have a direct responsibility to the public that they are serving to punish according to the law. There should be no question that the specific purpose of the law is to punish criminals. Whether punishment is effective or not, and whether there are mitigating circumstances or not, are not issues in these cases. The courtroom is not the place for Christian generosity. The courtroom is the place to punish as the law provides.

FORGIVENESS

Prior to examining the practical role of forgiveness, let's look briefly at the concept of atonement. The idea of the sacrifice of blood, particularly human blood, to appease the gods is as ancient as superstition itself. The idea that the sacrifice of human blood for the remission of the sins of all of humanity is as barbaric as any other form of human sacrifices. Jesus was actually executed as a criminal, but the authors of the Bible chose to characterize his death as a blood sacrifice. This instance is particularly sick because the god in question arranged the sacrifice of his own son to himself to compensate for his own error in the design of man. It assumes that man is inherently evil; that his every thought and act is evil. We do not accept that proposition. Perhaps all men have evil ideas at times, but most men don't act upon those ideas most of the time. Most men think and act in a just manner most of the time. Some men might think and act justly all of the time. Atonement, the forgiveness by a third party, be it a god or a priest, for sins against man, is a crime against the just and good man. It is the betrayal of the just to the unjust. Atonement is the bane of civilization.

It's interesting that forgiveness as a rule of personal conduct is mentioned at all in the New Testament. If a good follower of the faith made no judgments, he would have nothing to forgive. But we do make judgments, and our concern is whether forgiveness is a valid concept within our group. We must begin with the knowledge that the act under consideration to be forgiven was harmful, and that it is in the interest of each individual, and of the group, that harmful acts are prevented or at the least minimized. We will grant that "to err is human", but we will insist that doing so is a personal choice. There is nothing about human nature that forces one to commit harmful acts. What then is the role of forgiveness, and whose role is it?

To forgive a wrong has personal and social consequences. We are evaluating how we should respond to a harmful action that was taken by someone. If we simply forgive every wrong action without question, we sanction that wrong action and we set the stage for more, probably continuous wrong actions from the same and other perpetrators. So we see that we have a responsibility to ourselves and to our community to not give blanket, unquestioning forgiveness at any time.

A good place to begin is with the perpetrator. Has he talked to us about the offense? Has he admitted to us personally that he has wronged us? Has he stated what his intentions were? Has he admitted that the act was intentional; not that he just made a mistake or that he couldn't help himself? Has he admitted that he deserves our contempt? Has he promised that he will never do that again? Has he asked to be forgiven? All of these questions are the responsibility of the offender to address, and if he fails to address each of them with us, we have absolutely no obligation and no right to forgive him.

A simple, "I'm sorry" or simpler, "Sorry", just doesn't meet the requirement. What do those words mean to most people? Usually they mean just a tiny bit more than nothing at all. They're just words that fall from the mouths of thoughtless people who do thoughtless, damaging things that they forget about as soon as the words evaporate into the air. If we have been wronged to the point that forgiveness is an issue, we can't accept this shorthand variety of penitence.

We must address the seriousness of the offense. Have we been slighted, or have we suffered permanent harm? Each situation of course stands on its own, but we owe it to ourselves, to our community and to our relationship with the person who has harmed us to give due weight and deliberation to any and all harmful acts. The offended is in a position of power, and such a position has sole responsibility for the quality of future relations with the offender.

Do we want to forgive repeated offenses? Has the offender apologized to us for the same offense more times than we care remember? We would think that there is a point where we would say, "No more. We can't have a relationship." Unfortunately there are those that we encounter who place less value on our relationship with them than they do on their undesirable whims. We should be able to recognize this in time to minimize their negative impact upon our lives. The sooner we do so, the less pain we will suffer from their lack of sensitivity to our needs.

There are situations when we have a clear understanding of the circumstances that could lead another person to wrong us. Perhaps we have done something similar ourselves, or we have at least thought about doing something like that, and as a result we actually feel a sort of kinship with the offender. We can sometimes be sympathetic, or at least empathetic with that person. We might rationalize that a lot of people do the same thing so we shouldn't be too tough on the offender. We might even feel varying degrees of compassion toward the offender, and as a result, we might find it quite easy to forgive. These and a variety of other reasons can come into play and tend to mitigate our reaction to the wrong and the wrongdoer. Many say that if you're compassionate, forgiveness is very easy.

These appeals are no doubt true whether they come from within or from a neutral observer. Careful examination reveals however that all of these situations simply beg to find a reason to forgive. This is not the same as saying that the wrong deserves our forgiveness. The fact that most automobile drivers would drive dangerously if they had no fear of getting a ticket, is not an excuse for everybody to drive dangerously. A wrong is still a wrong, and when it is an act of volition, there is no excuse for it regardless of how common it might be. As a society we pay police officers to write tickets in order to assure some degree of safety on our highways. As individuals we are obliged to write personal tickets to preserve some degree of our personal safety and happiness.

There are selfish reasons to forgive. The most obvious perhaps is that forgiving can win the favor of someone, and the value of someone's favor can influence how willing we are to forgive. This can be very unrefined as when forgiveness is the tradeoff for some immediate gain. This is simply trading. It isn't pretty, but it happens, and it is the prerogative of the offended.

When people talk about forgiveness being very easy when you are compassionate, they are actually talking about a position of power. Compassion is the grown up word for pity. So when we forgive from a position of compassion, aren't we looking down on this poor helpless person who couldn't prevent himself from injuring us? Aren't we declaring that he is weak and that we are stronger than he is? Aren't we declaring our superiority over this person who we think will be miserable without our forgiveness? Compassion can be valuable, but we must not forget its source.

Forgiveness can be a vehicle to peace of mind. It's a way to put the past behind us so we can get on with our lives. It can get the irritation, anger and pain out of our system. We can set aside the wrong done and allow ourselves to focus on more positive things. It can remove the mental load that was dragging us down from harboring anger and hate. These are all benefits to us if we can forgive with a high level of trust that the wrong will not reoccur.

We are usually very willing to forgive someone who is very dear to us. The very best relationships will experience some affronts and some wrongs. If we are rational, we will easily forgive many of these because the relationship is more valuable to us than harboring ill will. But we must acknowledge the fact that good relationships are based upon the fact that a lot of good things outweigh some minor negative things. If our relationship encounters a lot of negative things, its value to us diminishes accordingly. In that case it is no longer a good relationship, and it is no longer a value to us. If we are rational, we will break off the relationship.

Forgiveness is a very personal matter, and it is reasonable to state that any rational act of forgiveness is essentially selfish. It's rational to forgive if doing so is good for the person doing it. It's irrational to forgive if doing so opens the door to pain or loss. Man should feel no guilt by refusing to forgive harmful actions that were volitional.

ALTRUISM

John the Baptist said, "He that hath two coats, let him impart to him that hath none; and he that hath meat, let him do likewise." In "Acts" chapter 2 verses 44 and 45 we are instructed, "And all that believed were together, and had all things common; And sold their possessions and goods, and parted them to all men, as every man had need." Karl Marx wrote "—only then can the narrow horizon of bourgeois right be crossed in its entirety and society inscribe on its banners: From each according to his ability, to each according to his needs!"(1) The modern altruist instructs us that the wealthy have a moral duty to "give back" to society. The implication being that they took their wealth from society. We will see that this is not the case, and that with very few exceptions, they acquired their wealth by providing the individuals who make up our society with the things that they wanted or needed.

Of the sources above, only Marx attempted to justify the altruist mentality, and he failed to do so even though he did succeed at wrongly vilifying capitalism. John doesn't ask why one has two coats and another has no coat. He doesn't know if the owner of two worked into the late hours of many nights to make a second coat, and he doesn't know if he who had no coat had traded his away for the services of a whore. New Testament scripture gives no justification for its multiple appeals to altruism and socialism. Borrowing from scripture and Marx, the modern altruist will have us believe that the need of others is all the justification that is required in order to bully the creators of wealth to be sacrificed to the poor. No altruist was, and no altruist is, interested in why there are differences of wealth among individuals. More importantly, *no altruist has ever justified why one man should be sacrificed to another man.* He just insists that it is right for those who have to give to those who need. He doesn't tell us why it's right because he can't.

Altruism cannot be justified in any form or from any perspective. Its basic concept, the sacrifice of the producers to the non-producers, is immoral. Every social experiment with it of any magnitude has failed because it is contrary to man's nature, his pursuit of his own self-interest, even enlightened self-interest. It also fails due to the other side of man's nature, his pursuit of reward without effort. The accurately stated practical application of altruism amounts to: from each according to his willingness to work and to each according to his wants and demands.

Several months ago I put the following question to my respective U.S. Senators and to my Representative in the House. "By what moral authority or if you prefer, by what system of values, does the government take money from one citizen and transfer it to another citizen? A brief and direct response will be appreciated." Unlike other letters that received a relatively timely, though usually vague, response from these lawmakers, only one of those honorable gentlemen responded to this request. He stated, "I believe that there is no moral authority that makes it possible." He is absolutely correct, and if there is no moral authority, the government that does it is immoral. The other lawmakers haven't responded, and they won't because they can't. There is no moral authority for State Altruism, Socialism or Communism. State welfare has the same moral authority as did the legendary Robin Hood, (robbing hoodlum) none. That is true regardless of the degree of need of the poor, regardless of the amount of wealth of the citizenry, and regardless of the amount of envy toward the rich.

Practicing Christians and by name only Christians have been Socialized, i.e., converted to Socialism without their knowing it. Even in the

United States, the country least infected by its Euro-Christian ancestry, the immoral concept of altruism, i.e., Socialism, Communism and Welfare Statism is alive and well. Most of us don't think of ourselves in those terms, however that is because we fail to recognize that there is no fundamental difference between the four concepts. There are differences of implementation and practice between Hitler and Stalin and other altruists, but the fundamental concept of John the Baptist is the tool for all of them. And though their tool may seem admirable to the casual observer, it is not; just as their motives were not and are not today. State sponsored/mandated altruism was and is the natural outcome for people who have been indoctrinated with the ideal of self-sacrifice for their entire life. The Bible does exactly that from Cain to the book of Acts.

The argument for altruism is as simple as John's statement: If you have two and I don't have any, you should give me one. It assumes that I need and want what you have, and that you have a moral obligation to give me what I need. Your act of giving half of your wealth to me will make our society better. You will have done "good", and I will be grateful to you forever. Or maybe I won't be so grateful. After all, am I not entitled to your wealth? It assumes that if you have more than I have then you have too much. It assumes that if I don't have what you have then I don't have enough. It assumes that you don't deserve all of the wealth that you have, and that I am poor for reasons beyond my control. It assumes that I will suffer if you don't help me, and that I shouldn't be allowed to suffer if you can prevent it.

Altruism states at its most fundamental level that you and I should share equally in whatever wealth exists between us. It has no concern about why you have more than I do in the first place. This basic idea carried Lenin into power. The fact that the social ideal of communism was never realized isn't important. The popular appeal of the idea is what made Lenin and Stalin possible, and it is the appeal of the idea that continues to attract its advocates and disarm its victims. If we simply look at its basic assumptions, we should instantly discern that the assumptions are wrong, and that its goal is immoral. We should also be clear that communism didn't fail just because Stalin didn't manage it right. It failed because it is morally wrong. It's morally wrong because it contradicts man's fundamental nature and the truth.

Man's fundamental nature is to pursue his own happiness, and the truth is that one person's need for something does not constitute a moral claim to it. We must be crystal clear about this one fact: my need for something does not constitute any obligation of any kind for you to supply it regardless of your ability to do so. Even if my life literally depends upon your help, you do not have a moral duty to help me. Your own happiness is your moral duty. If saving my life will make you happier, then, and only then should you do so.

Since human life is at the core of our value system, it's necessary to digress for just a moment. Each individual pursues a particular career in order to provide for their own needs for existence and happiness. In a free society, each of us trades our particular service for the services of others. Doctors happen to be in the business of health care. The fact that they have chosen that particular career does not make them slaves to the needs of every person that needs medical help. Medical help, although vital to life, is not an entitlement. It is a service that is provided at great personal expense in terms of time and study by individuals who have as much of a claim to their own lives as do attorneys and truck drivers to theirs. Their business should be governed by the rules of voluntary trade just like any other service. Medical professionals have no more moral duty to sacrifice their lives than do the practitioners of any other profession or trade.

There are some people who appear to derive a great deal of personal satisfaction from helping others, and some that actually dedicate their entire lives to doing so. Their lives are literally a mission of mercy. Their happiness appears to be the product of their activity. If they pursue this activity by their personal choice, and if they find happiness in doing so, we cannot take issue with their choice. We would only hope that they are rewarded by their activity now rather than in some future existence.

We cannot be so kind to the professional altruist whether he is a politician wielding the power to tax and redistribute, or some person lobbying for tax dollars to do his brand of good deed. These people are help addicts that find personal power and gratification in spending other peoples money to sponsor every imaginable benefit for the "victims" and the "unfortunate" of society. They perpetuate and exploit class warfare for their personal benefit. They enjoy the power they have over those who supply the money and those who are the beneficiaries of their benevolence, and they manipulate both so they can perpetuate their activity. They measure their self-worth by how successful they are at this evil activity. Their activities are unjust unless we believe in the justice of John the Baptist, which is simply this: any person with any need has a moral claim to the life of any person who can satisfy their need. That is not justice. That is parasitism, and the advocates of altruism should know it.

We said earlier that Americans have been Socialized or converted to Socialism although we don't think of ourselves as Socialists. We must realize that Socialism is a political philosophy. It isn't about the color of our flag or what our political parties call themselves. Socialism is about sacrificing individual rights in favor of group rights, and that translates into the power of the state over the individual activities of the people.

Are we not socialized? Do we not believe that the state has the proper right and the moral authority to tax our earnings and property in order to fund a whole galaxy of "good" programs? Have we not moved from that first little public welfare program known as Social Security, which arguably started the disintegration of the family, to Medicare, Medicaid, food stamps, public housing, public swimming pools, public golf courses, publicly funded sports arenas, and whatever else is deemed to be for the public good? Do we not routinely send a major portion of our income to the public treasury where most of it is used to fund programs that many of us seldom or never use? We are gradually sacrificing ourselves to the power of the state. The mandate of John the Baptist, the teachings of the apostles of Jesus and the philosophy of Karl Marx are the pattern of our sacrifice.

Need does not constitute a moral claim to anything. Need does not justify the mandate of John. Need does not justify Marxism or any of its corollary isms. Need does not justify confiscation and redistribution by the welfare state. One test of a philosophy or an ideal is how willing is its advocate to live by it. It's worth noting that the most obvious advocates of altruism don't really believe in it. If they did, the high ranking religious officials, the high ranking charity officials and the high ranking public officials would all live much more modestly than they do. They would direct that any wealth or income beyond their basic needs would be given to those in need. Their example does not speak well for the idea of "from each according to his ability."

The self styled moralist tells us that caring for others is what differentiates us from the other animals. That is not true. Possessing a rational mind is what differentiates us from other animals, and a rational mind has the responsibility and the right to evaluate and to decide for itself. A rational mind is not subject to the whims and will of the pack to which it happens to belong. A rational mind is not required to sacrifice itself because of the need of some other rational mind, and nobody can honestly and accurately state that it has a moral duty to do so. Caring, giving, helping and sharing are not moral or ethical or "right" obligations. The need of one person in no way constitutes a claim to the property of any other person. The state has the authority of power to confiscate the wealth of one citizen for the benefit of another citizen, but it has no moral authority to do so.

There is nothing intrinsically wrong with charity or with helping others. We all know people whom we assist financially or in some other way. There is nothing wrong with giving money to an acquaintance or to a relative if we want to do so. There is nothing wrong with shoveling snow for the elderly couple that lives down the street. There is nothing wrong with supporting a charitable organization that we are familiar with. There is nothing wrong with giving money to a beggar if we want to do so. These acts of charity are based upon personal good will. Good will acts of charity are exactly that, and they can only be good will acts if they are performed voluntarily. But it is absolutely wrong and immoral to not have the right to say no to any person, any cause or any organization. The right to say no is exactly what is taken away from us by the altruists of the welfare state. That is confiscation. That is the denial of our rights as an individual to determine what happens to the wealth that we produce.

Our money is that which we have earned by devoting a portion of our life to obtain it. So our money represents our time spent. Our time and our life are one and the same thing. They are synonymous. Anyone who tells us that the need of others constitutes a moral claim to any part of our life is a liar. Each man begins his slow but certain journey into serfdom when he first accepts that lie of John the Baptist. Charity is not a moral mandate. Charity is not a prerequisite of good citizenship. Charity is a gift whether in the form of money or of our time. A gift is given by choice not by force or coercion.

PART VI

The Altruist Ideal

GOOD INTENTIONS

After assuring me that the government has no moral authority to transfer wealth from one citizen to another citizen, my sole responding lawmaker went on to say:

> *"Taxes are allowed under the Constitution for the maintenance of a common defense, or military, and for maintaining our trade treaties. Every other government program should be based on whether or not it benefits society as a whole."*

The second sentence is similar to the Bible, it's soft wax, and like the Bible it can be twisted and stretched to suit the pleasure of any man that chooses to do so. That is precisely the kind of thinking that has allowed the out of control growth of the welfare state in the United States. Virtually any organized group and any experienced politician can make a "benefits society as a whole" argument for just about anything that can be imagined. The result is that there is no end to the potential list of "do good" government programs. That is the fundamental economic problem with the welfare state. It is essentially without rules. Anything that can be defined as a benefit to society as a whole, or for the general good becomes a candidate for a new or expanded government program. Every new or expanded government program deprives the individual citizen of the right to make his own economic decisions.

Those who make the rules, legislators who are strongly swayed, if not totally controlled by various special interests walk a narrow line. In their efforts to satisfy the requests of the special interest groups that put up the money to fund their election coffers, our legislators must be wary that they don't anger their constituents with so much tax that a tax revolt develops. They realize that the producers, those who work and pay taxes, are the key to the success of the state welfare game. They realize that there would be no wealth to confiscate if the producers decided that they are just as well off if they chose to not produce and to join those on the welfare roles, or better yet, to join the underground economy. The first option of course has already been exercised by thousands of people who were once employed at lower income jobs. They have realized that they are better off on government welfare than they would be if they continued to work. The second group has chosen to protect themselves from the do-gooders in another way. Our legislators must be cautious not to be so greedy that large numbers of producers will be encouraged to join either of these groups.

Most people of course continue to work. They continue to be the victims of the altruist machine of the welfare state. Many do so grudgingly because they are aware of the injustice that is forced upon them, yet they are still better off than they would be on welfare. Many others do so because they have been trained to believe in the virtue of altruism, the virtue of self-sacrifice in the name of "the good".

The four quotations that follow are a continuation of my lawmaker's response.

> *"I believe very strongly in reducing the amount and size of government programs, and in abolishing the welfare state that has been built up over the last century."*

Abolishing the welfare state will require rethinking and abandoning the proposition that the government should have any involvement in any program that "benefits society as a whole." The purpose of government is to protect the life and the rights of its citizens, not to feed, clothe and house them. When government assumes the role of provider it becomes a self-contradiction because the only way that it can provide for some is to take by force from others. It must do evil to the producers in order to do good for the non-producers. It drags down its own strength in order to sustain its weakness. It encourages and nurtures the parasite that will eventually destroy its fundamental strength.

Like the vast majority of our lawmakers in Washington, this writer's congressman is a well-educated and reasonably intelligent person. We must pose the question then, how can such a person take the position that the government should support soft wax definitions of programs that benefit society as a whole, and at the same time "believe strongly in reducing the amount and size of government programs, and abolishing the welfare state"? A fundamental contradiction lies therein. It is the same genre of contradiction whereby a government created to protect the life and rights of its citizens routinely confiscates the wealth of its producers in order to support the lives of its non-producers. How can any reasonably intelligent, well-educated person support these contradictions? Wouldn't it be refreshing if just one of our representatives to congress stood up and denounced altruism as a fraud and a contradiction of the purpose of a government of free people? That would be a good beginning for a congressman that "believes strongly in abolishing the welfare state."

> *"Yes, the less fortunate should be assisted, but they should receive their assistance from the generosity of the good people of this nation, voluntarily helping their fellow man, not being forced into 'compassion' by the federal government."*

Yes. This is right on the target. Reasonable assistance can only be given by one who has enough knowledge of a particular situation that he can determine how much and what kind of assistance, if any, should be given. Sometimes we must rely on an agency to do that for us, but not a government agency. Lending assistance is generous, but we are not required to give assistance in order to be "good." Forced compassion is neither good nor generous. It is immoral.

"Many government programs are fraught with fraud and abuse, and they must be brought into compliance."

Not many, but most, perhaps all government programs are fraught with fraud. That's just one more reason for minimizing the scope of the government. We should expect fraud any time that people are put into a position where they can spend other people's money. This is particularly true when we are talking about the amount of money that goes through the federal treasury. After all, the bureaucrats handling that money are just as selfish as the rest of mankind, and when we're talking about more than 4.6 billions of dollars spent daily, a few hundred million that goes astray every day doesn't seem like very much.

Can we even imagine what it would require to bring all government programs into compliance? If we are talking about all of the fraud and graft that is associated with spending billions of dollars daily, thinking that even fifty percent of the fraud and graft could be eliminated is as absurd as the Bible. To bring all government programs into compliance would require a whole new department of government, and it would of necessity have to be a huge one at that. That's the last thing that we need. Even if that were done, fraud and graft would continue. But we are going astray here. Our concern is whether the government should tax one citizen in order to provide for the existence of another citizen.

"I believe in helping the needy but not the greedy."

That is the lawmaker's personal choice. Helping is not a moral mandate, and as he stated, it is not the proper role of the government.

There are many people who see the world of capitalism as one that is filled with unjust inequality. Their view is that there are many thousands of people that are entrapped in poverty: children, single moms, some elderly, physically or mentally disadvantaged, and those living in the ghettos. They see these people as victims of our society. They believe that these people are poor because of the way that our society and our economic system operate. They believe in their hearts that society has a moral responsibility to help them. They believe that the rich if left to their own devices will never help as much as they should help. They believe that if society gets the right direction from the government that most of these people can be helped to attain their particular vision of justice. They pressure the government to direct society in ways that they believe will accomplish their ends.

The government sees the poor only as economic units. Its actions to correct the injustices of society focus primarily, although not exclusively, on equal opportunity for education, equal opportunity for employment, and "temporary financial assistance" for virtually all of life's necessities until such time as the poor are able to provide for themselves in the unfair world of capitalism. The government view of these economic units is that they will gladly go in the direction that the government is trying to direct them to go in if their fellow citizens will foot the bill to get them there. We must assume that "there" is when they no longer depend upon the sweat of their fellow citizens to sustain their survival. They will become successful economic units that will then be able to help support other unsuccessful economic units. We also must assume that all but some of the elderly and the seriously disadvantaged are expected to become successful economic units.

Part of the argument to gain public support for these welfare programs is that the rich people of our country have too much money, and that they don't do, or wouldn't do, enough to help the poor if the government didn't make them do so. We wonder who decides what is too much money. We also wonder who is going to invest money into the companies that are going to provide jobs for us if the rich don't do it. And we state again that the rich have no moral obligation to take care of the poor. There is no moral/ethical basis for taxation and redistribution of wealth. The peddlers of altruism have never been able to state one. This practice of the government has the same moral/ethical authority as the fundamental political philosophy of Karl Marx: one person's need constitutes a just claim to the labor and resources of any-body capable of relieving that need.

Reported income is the government's essential device for deciding who is poor and who is not poor. It does not take into account net worth and unreported income. Therefore we have many of thousands of people who have substantial assets but limited income that are classi-fied as poor. It is no secret to the government that there are many other thousands of people who have significant unreported income, and they too could be classified as poor. Much unreported income, that from the so-called underground economy, is the direct result of the heavy taxation rate that is needed to finance the government welfare pro-grams. Therefore the excessive taxation required to fund the welfare state encourages many otherwise honest citizens to hide some or all of their income. This necessitates even higher rates of taxation upon other citizens. Finally we have many thousands of people that are actually poor. The beneficiaries of the welfare state are a combination of people with various levels of assets, people who fail to report part or all of their income, and the truly poor. The government does not support any of them. They are all are supported by taxpayers.

Taxes are only paid by those people who report their income, and the vast majority of taxpayers are anything but rich. Most taxpayers actually have to budget very carefully in order to meet their monthly financial obligations, and many of them have little or no discretionary income. The basic needs of many taxpayers are compromised by the fact that they pay taxes, some of which is sent to families that are actu-ally in better financial condition than they are. In many cases the gov-ernment literally takes food off the table of some of the non-poor in order to put it on the table of the poor, and many of the poor are not actually poor, and many of them are frauds. This problem is not the result of fraud. Fraud is inherent in government programs. The real problem is due to the fact that most Americans believe in the alleged ravings of that madman in the wilderness, John the Baptist, and that it is the proper business of the government to transfer wealth from one citizen to another.

The wealthiest five-percent of Americans foot the bill for about fifty-five-percent of the federal government. The working middle class pays the balance of it. The argument is often made that the rich should pay more in order to minimize the tax burden on the middle class. We must admit that the very wealthy could probably do so with minimal or no effect upon their lifestyle. But the critical issue is not about whom pays the bills. The issue is about what the bills are for. The critical point is that taxation and redistribution in all of its forms is unjust and immoral.

It's apparent that government programs to solve the problems of the poor are fraught with problems and injustice. Many of the poor are not really poor. Many of those who really are poor, and who have no physical or mental impairments, lack and will always lack, that mysterious something inside of them that they need in order to even believe that they can become self-sufficient economic units. If some did actually believe it, there is no way to determine if they are willing to discipline themselves in order to accomplish that goal. There is no way for the government to identify any of these types. Essentially the government is totally in the dark in terms of determining who actually needs help and who will actually use help to attain the assumed goal. Finally there is the necessity to tax hundreds of thousands of citizens that are actually poor themselves in order to conduct this immoral business.

MEANS AND ENDS

Underlying its evaluation and treatment of its economic units lies the assumption of the government that given adequate means, the poor will be lifted up from poverty and become financially successful. As we said earlier, the focus is on providing an adequate education and a level playing field in the employment arena. This should give all people the opportunity to earn an adequate income, and with that they should be economically successful. We have a micro-society within our society where we can actually get an idea as to whether this assumption is true. In fact our micro-society has the ideal of many altruists: equal outcomes, at least in terms of income. It actually has equal pay for unequal performance. Our micro-society is virtually every enlisted barracks of virtually every facility of our armed forces.

In order to keep our playing field totally level, let's assume that our barracks is for some type of technical training. Its occupants have just completed basic training, and they are going to spend the next fifteen weeks learning their specialty. They completed basic training with various levels of success, but they all have the same pay grade. They are all fully equipped in terms of military gear and supplies. They all receive the same clothing allowance that will permit them to maintain and replace their uniforms as needed. They all have access to the mess hall. They are all unmarried. Essentially all of their income is discretionary.

We will observe early on that all of these individuals (economic units) have various personal preferences. Some of them take their meals at the mess hall twenty-one times a week. Some do so except on weekends when they are off base. Some only eat at the mess for breakfast or for lunch. Some never eat at the mess. They all get enough to eat, but some prefer to have a burger and a beer at the Enlisted Club than to eat that "slop" at the mess hall.

We will also notice that off-duty time is spent in various ways. Some spend most of their spare time in the barracks studying, writing letters, shooting a little pool or watching the tube. Some will take in the base movie now and then or check out some sporting gear for a little free recreation off the base. Some will get involved in some base sponsored sports competition. Some will take correspondence courses or attend night classes at a local school or college. Some will work a part time civilian job. Some will just sort of hang out in the barracks.

We only see some of these individuals at reveille and during duty hours. Being around the barracks is a total waste to them, and they have no interest in sports activities. We'll usually find them at the E-club on weeknights where they hang out with their buds, drink some beers, and eat some pizza. They talk the talk, watch the game on television and bet a few bucks on the outcome of the game. They usually get back to the barracks after the lights are out. They make more noise than they should as they stumble in and out of the latrine, and then they literally fall into what they hope is their own bunk.

Some of these individuals disappear every weekend that they don't have duty. The bars in town are more fun than the E-club, and there are lots of local chicks that like to drink, dance and have a good time. It doesn't take them long to find one that will shack with them for Friday and Saturday night. All our guys need to do is to buy the booze and a little food. If all goes well, they report on time for training on Monday morning.

We notice other differences as time passes. Some of our guys acquire pretty nice civilian wardrobes, nice jewelry, tattoos and cars. We wonder how some of them can afford all of the stuff that they have. We especially wonder how a few of them can afford new cars. We wonder also how the guys that drop twenty bucks at the E-club every night can afford the clothes, the cars and their off base activities.

We notice one day that "A" isn't wearing his watch. He tells us that he had to pawn it for a few days. We never see him wear it again. Didn't he say that his mom gave it to him when he graduated from high school? Not too long after that we notice that he's not wearing his high school ring. There's a rumor that one of the guys in the barracks is a lender. His deal is three bucks for two loaned for seven days or less. It's two bucks for one loaned for eight to fifteen days, and no loans for more than fifteen days. It's strictly against regulations, but we know it's happening, and "A" is borrowing from him. The word is that if you borrow from the lender he is the first guy you see on payday, and the last thing you want to do is tell anybody about his loan business. We hear that the lender is putting over a thousand bucks in the bank every payday.

Some guys in the barracks are missing some of their personal things. This has been going on for several weeks now. "A" isn't doing well in class lately. His efficiency has dropped from number two in the class to number eighteen. Training is interrupted one morning when the M.P. come in. They want to talk to "A" for a couple of minutes. He doesn't return to class. His court martial doesn't go well for him. As though doing time and losing his stripe wasn't bad enough, he's been told that his chick is pregnant. He's not sure if the baby is his, but he assumes so. Damn the luck. He wonders what else could go wrong.

The M.P. were talking to the lender last week. Nothing happened, but "A" took a terrible fall in the latrine at the brig. They transferred him to sick bay for four days. His brig time set him too far back in class. He's been dropped from training and assigned to a guard unit someplace.

The actions of the character types described above are totally real. If we could actually live within a military barracks, we would be very likely to witness very similar behaviors. "A" and the lender represent the two extremes of personal economic management. We observe that there are some in the barracks that approximate "A", and there are some that approximate the lender. Some live beyond their means while some live well within their means. Some live exactly at the level of their means. Our purpose was to demonstrate that people not only can, but that they absolutely will, end up in totally different economic situations regardless of their capacity to earn. Virtually anybody who has spent a year in the regular military could verify the actuality of this scenario.

We will see very similar economic outcome extremes if we simply take the time to observe the behavior of family, friends and business associates. Some do quite well economically. Some are continually in debt and struggling to make ends meet. We will see both extremes at virtually all levels of income. We must conclude that economic outcomes are more the result of personal choices than they are of personal income. How well people get by is the result of how well they prioritize their needs and their wants. With the possible exception of the very wealthy, we can be certain that the reason that some people can afford everything that they need is because they have made it a practice not to buy everything that they want.

It is not our purpose to pass judgment upon the activities of anybody. Outside of breaking the law, how they choose to live their lives is their personal affair. We simply want to point out that actions always have consequences, and that many actions have predictable consequences. It is not our business to define which consequences are right for any other person.

POLITICS

The welfare state has been with us in America for so long now, that the majority of our citizens can't remember anything else. Nurtured by the Christian ethic of self-sacrifice, we have gradually evolved away from the belief in responsibility and self-reliance that dominated our economic thinking prior to the advent of Social Security. Since then, and particularly since the advent of "the great society", we have come to accept the notion that any problem or inconvenience of every "disadvantaged" person as defined by congress or the courts, is the responsibility of all persons who are not disadvantaged. By virtue of blindly accepting that proposition, we routinely allow the government to confiscate more and more of our income and allow it to be redistributed by myriad and mindless government bureaucracies.

Each election year, and particularly during general elections, our leaders and potential leaders debate the tax issue to various degrees. Though some will argue that our citizens might be overtaxed and make promises to reduce or at least not to increase the tax burden, none of them so much as hint that it is wrong for the government to be an agent for the transfer of wealth. There is no longer any debate about the legitimacy or the illegitimacy of this practice. The only debate is regarding how much of the wealth of the producers should be confiscated for the benefit of "the needy" and the bureaucracies that serve them. In fairness to our politicians we must state that it would be political suicide to suggest that the government should abandon these programs. Such a person would be branded with every imaginable derogative by every altruist in the country, and virtually every citizen would now agree with them. That is because we have come to accept the welfare state as good, and that is because we have never stopped to evaluate the immoral mandate of John the Baptist and later Christian leaders.

THE ECONOMIC UNIT

The government is not amiss in its view of us as economic units. Our family and friends view us as something more than that as we would hope that they would, but all of living existence, including human existence, is essentially about economics. The fundamental issue of survival is about economics as is the fundamental issue of reproduction. The purpose of every species of plant and every species of animal appears to be to exist and to reproduce. Every species requires specific nourishment and protection in order to do so. Those specific requirements constitute the economics of their existence, and if those economic conditions are met, they will be successful at existing and reproducing. The same is true for the human species. The only differences being that human beings demand a reason for its being so, and they can choose whether or not to do the things that are necessary in order to do so. All other animals live by instinct. The human animal must make decisions about the multitude of choices that confront him, and virtually every decision is an economic one.

The focus of altruists and their agents in government is generally limited to assuring that the poor are subsidized financially. But as we observed in our barracks community, income does not assure that a person will not be poor. Individual choices about virtually all of life's activities determine economic outcomes. This is a fact whether we are looking at life in a barracks, life in a ghetto, or life in a middle income suburb. We will observe successful and unsuccessful economic units in every type of economic environment. We will find individuals that are consistently moving toward a better life in every ghetto. We will find individuals that are consistently moving toward poverty in every middle income community. The difference in economic outcomes is driven by individual choices. The human animal, lacking the instinctive ability to take automatic survival actions, must choose actions from a variety that are available to him. He needs knowledge of as many possible actions as possible and the likely outcomes of each in order to make successful survival (economic) choices.

It is not the business of one man to determine which consequences are right for another man, but it would be appropriate to advise another man of available alternatives and their probable outcomes. It seems reasonable that the appropriate function of the public education system would be to demonstrate to its pupils that they are economic units, that virtually all actions are economic actions, and that specific actions have specific consequences. Some people will no doubt argue that our children need to be taught more than that. They need to learn how to be a whole person, a caring person, a responsible person, an honest person, etc. All of those goals are worthy, but we must honestly state that being a successful economic unit is the prerequisite to a successful existence.

When we, parents as well as teachers, think about teaching our young people about economics, we're not thinking about a course study in Econ 101. We're simply looking for a way to help them to know what we know about being a successful economic unit. We want them to know that they will be making economic decisions every hour of every day for the rest of their lives, and that they have no instincts that will make the right decisions for them. We want them to know that whatever their goals are in life, that there are specific things that will take them in that direction, and there are specific things that will deter them from getting there. We want them to know that virtually every decision that they make is an economic decision.

Many of the things that they need to know about personal economics are not found in most textbooks. Responsible sex education is not even permitted in many public schools, but it is one of the most important things that young people need to know about personal economics. This is not surprising on two counts. The schools give extremely little instruction of any kind regarding personal economics, and many people are positively horrified if the word "sex" is used in any context with people under the age of eighteen years or with people of the opposite sex of any age. The big "S" word actually paralyzes the thought system of many people whenever they hear it. It seems that the fruit of the tree of ignorance is preferred to the fruit of the tree of knowledge of good and evil. We must ask, "If irresponsible sex is immoral, isn't it also immoral to fail to give instruction about responsible sex? Would we prefer to find a hundred used condoms on the school steps or see one child born into a life of poverty?"

Our purpose in this book is to point out the evil of altruism, not to define what is right and wrong with our education system. But since poverty, particularly the poverty of children, is the engine of the welfare state, we would be remiss to renounce the welfare state without offering at least a suggestion about what to do about poverty. We must acknowledge up front however that poverty has been a part of human existence throughout recorded history and probably forever. If there were a cure-all it would have surely been found before now. From what we observe about human behavior, poverty is probably inevitable for some as long as each individual is free to choose his own path. Only a dictator would advocate taking that freedom away even if for such a worthy cause as eliminating poverty. What we will offer then is only one possibility, and it would certainly yield mixed results.

It's questionable whether many young people really think about being wealthy or even upper middle class. It's questionable whether many have any aspirations at all about being non-poor. It's questionable whether many have economic aspirations that go beyond a pizza and a coke for today's lunch. But it's reasonable to assume that most young people at least have a sense that they don't want to be poor. So perhaps it would be appropriate to approach our subject from a "how not to be poor" perspective. That is actually a negative however, so a more powerful approach would actually be to instruct them about "how to be poor". Most of the instruction could simply be based upon what we know as adults, what we have personally experienced or witnessed. So what follows will serve only as a primer for parents and teachers that think there might be some merit in educating our young people about the economics of existence.

BASIC INSTRUCTION ON HOW TO BE POOR

Since you think that you might want to be poor, it's important that you know what the fundamentals of poverty are. You should only proceed with the instruction after you understand what poverty is, and that you are certain that you still want to be poor.

Being poor means that you don't have enough of the things that your body requires to exist in a healthy condition. It does not mean that you just can't have a burger, fries and a soft drink whenever you feel like it. It means that there is not enough food of any kind available to you to maintain your body in good health. It means that your body is actually degenerating due to a lack of adequate nutrition. It is slowly withering away.

Being poor means that you don't have adequate clothing to protect your body from the elements. It does not mean that you just can't afford to buy some of the nice clothing items that you would like to have. Being poor is not about not having nice things, its about not having the basic things you need in order to be protected from the freezing cold, the pouring rain and from the burning sun. Being poor means that your body is in jeopardy of being injured by the elements because you don't have the resources to protect it.

Being poor is about not having adequate shelter. It's about living in some kind of shelter without adequate protection from the elements, or one that is so crowded with other poor people that there is no place for you to call your own. If you have a bed, you probably share it with one or two or three others. Chances are that you have to sleep on the floor, and if you're lucky you will have a few rags to try to keep warm with. The bathroom, if there is one, is always busy. The demand for hot water is greater than is provided. Personal toilet items are virtually non-existent. Bathroom privacy isn't a consideration. Getting and staying clean is almost impossible.

There you have the basics of being poor. Individual circumstances will vary, but the above conditions are common to many poor people. The following rules are intended to assist you in accomplishing your goal of being poor. Poverty is assured if you follow all of them. The first five rules are the most important, and if you will just add a nice mixture of some of the other rules to the first five, you are assured of reaching your goal.

Rule 1. <u>Never take responsibility for any part of your life.</u> You have every right to believe that everything that happens to you is beyond your control. Everything turns out badly no matter how hard you try to do well. You have every right to blame other people and outside forces for the infinite amount of ill fortune that you have experienced and continue to experience every day of your life. You are the victim of fate, the system and other people. Never stray from the belief that you are a victim.

Rule 2. <u>Have a new economic unit (a baby) that you can't afford.</u> New economic units are the quickest way to start you on your road to poverty. Their basic requirements: formula, food, diapers and medication will often be more costly than your own basic requirements. So if you are only borderline poor now, a new economic unit will quickly push you over the edge. New economic units provide additional advantages to you. They often don't sleep when you want them to, so they require you to be awake when you need to be getting some sleep of your own. This helps you to soon develop mental and physical fatigue. These two conditions are valuable because they can prevent you from making rational decisions at times. New economic units have five basic functions for the first seventeen thousand six hundred hours of their existence: they eat, cry, urinate, pass feces and spit up. These activities demand almost constant attention from you, and add to your mental and physical fatigue A new economic unit will be virtually totally dependent upon you for food, clothing, shelter and medical care for the first six thousand five hundred seventy days of its life. This fact will add to the probability that you will be able to remain poor for at least that long.

Rule 3. <u>Avoid getting an education.</u> Acquiring knowledge and how to use it is primarily for the purpose of learning how to operate within our social/economic system. You won't need those kinds of information if you want to be poor. Knowledge and how to use it is like having good tools to work with. You are more likely to be successful if you have good tools so it's vital to take all possible measures to avoid acquiring knowledge and the skill of using it.

Rule 4. <u>Never plan ahead.</u> All of your actions should be based upon spur of the moment whims. If you want to do something, do it now. If you want to get something, get it now. Planning ahead and thinking about what you might do in the future will surely detract from the gratification that you presently desire. Don't ever deny yourself gratification. Planning ahead can also be confusing. You might start thinking about being something other than being poor. If you do that, you might start taking actions that will prevent you from being poor. The best way to avoid that problem is to live every minute like it is your last one, and then you need have no concern about the future.

Rule 5. <u>Drink plenty of alcohol and/or use illegal drugs.</u> Alcohol and drugs serve two major functions that help to ensure your poverty. They are both expensive and therefore they use up some of the assets that you require to properly sustain your life. The biggest benefit is that they impair your brain from functioning properly. Man's brain is his

primary tool for survival. It guides man in all of his activities. Therefore, if you keep your brain impaired with alcohol or drugs, you prevent your body from operating at its best. At the very least, you will do
a lot of stupid things while your brain is impaired. You are also likely
to cause serious injury to yourself that could impair you for the rest of
your life. This is a big step toward permanent poverty.

Rule 6. <u>Day dream every chance that you get.</u> This is not to be confused with planning ahead. Day dreaming can actually hinder you
from planning ahead as long as you never get serious about fulfilling
your day dreams. Dream about being a movie star, a fashion designer, a
professional athlete, a novelist or a business tycoon. Dream that you
have some great talent that will be discovered, and that you will live a
life of luxury. Dream that you can have anything that you want and
that you don't have to do anything to get it.

Rule 7 <u>Waste whatever assets you do have.</u> Taking care of your
things, whatever their value, prolongs their use to you and postpones
the time that you will need to replace them. The need for frequent
replacement of the things that you need helps to assure that you will
never have the means to acquire something that you just want. Being
able to acquire wants is a sign of affluence, not of poverty. In addition
to not taking care of your things, you should waste food. If you are
responsible for utilities, you should be sure to use them to the fullest at
all times.

Rule 8. <u>Expect that you will always be poor.</u> This is like a safety
valve. If you expect to be poor, any notions that you may have about
not being poor will soon leave you. You will not be tempted to start
thinking ahead or about making any plans whatsoever about being
anything other than poor. If you ever waver from this rule, be sure to
talk with others who expect to be poor and who expect you to be poor.

Rule 9. <u>If you want to be poor, you must choose role models that
are poor, and you should make certain to hang out with poor people.</u>
This rule naturally follows rule 8. The poorer the person is the better
role model he or she will be for you. Associating exclusively with poor

people will ensure that you get the proper moral support that you will need in order to keep yourself on track in your effort to be truly poor. They will be valuable to remind you of the futility of thinking otherwise, and to offer assurance that you can't be anything other than poor even if you wanted to do otherwise. If you really want to be poor, do what other poor people do.

Rule 10. <u>Never seek employment.</u> You obviously don't want a reliable source of income if you want to be poor. If you are forced or coerced into seeking employment, and you are unfortunate enough to get a job, you can take a few simple steps to ensure that you are not successful. Employers hire people to perform certain tasks that are critical to the success of their company. If employees don't show up for work, the tasks don't get done so the employer must replace employees that don't come to work. Be absent as much as possible. Be late as much as possible. This isn't as good as being absent, but it causes enough disruption that if done regularly it will get you terminated. Be a minimal performer. Don't do one thing more than you are forced to do. If your performance is poor enough, your employer will probably replace you. Do shoddy work. The more mistakes you make, the better your chances of being replaced are. Be disruptive. Create problems for your co-workers and for your employer. This will increase the chances that your employer will replace you.

Rule 11. <u>Buy everything that you want, and be sure not to confuse your wants from your needs.</u> You will have reliable income if you aren't able to remain unemployed. All is not lost as a result. This rule and those that follow will keep you on the road to poverty even though you have reliable income. By spending your income on unessential wants rather than essential needs, you will still be deprived of those things that you need. You will still be technically poor even though you have income and a variety of toys or other non-essentials.

Rule 12. <u>Buy what you want on credit, and do so to the limits that are permitted by those who are willing to continue lending you money.</u> The ideal lender will allow you to repay a minimum balance, usually the monthly interest, forever. This means that in the long term, you can actually pay ten, twenty or even a hundred times more in interest charges than you were charged for the item that you purchased on credit. It's virtually impossible to find a better way to dispose of your income and to ensure that you have little to show for it.

Rule 13. <u>Gamble with your money.</u> Most gamblers lose. Most habitual gamblers lose a lot. Gambling establishments pay for their lavish facilities with the losses of the people that frequent them. The odds in the state lottery are even worse. The lure of winning millions of dollars has helped to keep millions of people poor by their betting millions of dollars that they will be the one in ten or fifty million to win. The chances of beating the local card shark or the local hustler are a little better, but if you are serious about being poor, any of these gambling opportunities are almost certain to help you to do so.

Rule 14. <u>Play on the guilt of your family and society.</u> They have been trained to believe that they are responsible for your inability to provide for yourself. Someone will provide you with at least the minimum needs for your survival. The government has the authority to take money from the producers and to transfer it to the non-producers. It has no qualms about sacrificing the producers to you in this way, and the producers have come to accept the idea of being sacrificial animals. Although this practice makes you a parasite that lives off the lives of your fellow citizens, you must not dwell upon that fact.

Rule 15. <u>Postpone as long as possible all decision making and taking action on necessary tasks.</u> This practice can create a state of mental overload and paralysis. It's virtually impossible to do anything of a constructive nature when you reach this state. If you do manage to take action on something, you are virtually assured of producing a poor result for your effort if you wait until the last possible minute to start.

Rule 16. <u>Review rules 1 through 5. Never take responsibility, have a new economic unit, avoid getting an education, don't plan ahead and drink lots of alcohol and use drugs.</u> These rules are the foundation of poverty. Be sure that you understand and practice them faithfully.

ALTRUISM VS. MORALITY

Let us suppose that a needy person were to hire a thug to coerce his neighbors into supporting him by the use of force or intimidation. Let as assume that there is no question about his need, and that there is no question about the ability of his neighbors to relieve his need. Can we accept the notion that his need justifies his actions? No! Can we accept the notion that this is a moral arrangement? No! His need, no matter how great, does not constitute a moral right for his actions. The ability of his neighbors to support him, regardless of their ability to do so, does not constitute a moral right for his actions. One person has no moral claim to any part of the wealth of any other person. No person has a moral claim to any part of the life of another person.

Now let's suppose that this same needy person, or his agent, can convince his representative in Congress that the government has the responsibility to sustain his life. His representative introduces a bill to that effect, and it is debated in Congress. Some representatives think that the bill is a good one. Some others disagree. After some time it is apparent that there is not enough support for the bill. Its advocates start to make deals with some of the representatives who do not favor the bill. Essentially they sell their votes for other legislation that they might or might not agree with in order to procure votes for the bill they want passed. Enough votes are bought or traded to get the bill passed.

We now have a law that makes the government responsible for the sustenance of its citizens. But since the government does not produce any wealth, it must take wealth from those of its citizens that do produce it. It is now legal for the government to confiscate some of the wealth of some of its citizens in order to support some of its other citizens. The needy person can now use the government to ensure his sustenance at the expense of his neighbors. It isn't legal because it is right. It isn't even legal because most of our representatives thought it was right. It is legal because some representative's votes were bought in order that they could get their own pet bill passed. Even if all legislators agreed that it was right, it is not. It is legal, but there is no moral/ethical justification for it.

Let's review the question posed to this writer's representatives in the United States Congress.

"By what moral authority or if you prefer, by what system of values, does the government take money from one citizen and transfer it to another citizen?"

Of three questioned, only one responded, and that response follows.

"I believe that there is no moral authority that makes it possible."

He was absolutely right. There is no moral authority that makes it possible. If it is not moral, is it immoral? Yes, absolutely! Unless we believe that there are actions that are neither moral nor immoral, these actions are immoral.

Now some will no doubt argue that the subject is not about morality, but about what is right. Such is simply an argument over semantics, not one of substance. For those who limit their understanding of moral actions to those defined by religious doctrine, we must state there can be no difference between what is right, what is just and what is moral within the entire realm of human relations. The imaginary situation above is a prime example. It would not be right, it would not be just and it would not be moral for one person to secure his existence through the use of force or intimidation upon his neighbors. If it is not right, it is not moral. If it is not just, it is not moral. If our representatives in government don't believe that there is a moral basis for the government to be the agent for the transfer of wealth between its citizens, they are fostering immoral activity by the government.

Does the government employ the use of force or intimidation in order to carry on its immoral activity? If we think in terms of armed agents coming to our door and threatening us, we would admit that it would be uncommon. However, there is no doubt in the minds of most citizens that failing to pay taxes will bring about unpleasant consequences. Those consequences vary widely and depend upon individual circumstances, all of which are less desirable to most citizens than paying the tax. There is little doubt that most citizens comply with the tax laws out of a sense of fear to one degree or another.

Some will argue that the tax laws and the redistribution of wealth are the will of the people. They claim that our elected officials reflect the will of the people, and that by virtue of the fact that they were elected by the majority of the people, the people are obliged to live by the laws that they enact. Only the last part is true. The people are obliged to live by the law. Of course that is true of every community and country in the world regardless of whether the law comes from an elected official or from a dictator.

The idea that the will of the majority is sacrosanct is erroneous. If ninety percent of Americans were atheists, it wouldn't justify banning religion in America. If ninety percent of Americans were vegetarians, it wouldn't justify banning meat in our diets. It should be obvious that a numerical majority is not the basis for determining what is right, just and moral.

Our government is a representative government, not a pure democracy. The majority elects representatives who are supposed to go to Washington to enact laws that will help to protect the lives and property of their constituents from domestic criminals and outlaw nations. These days a candidate might spend millions of dollars to inform his potential voters about what he will do for them as their representative. If a candidate today were totally honest, he or she would spend millions of dollars to inform voters of the following.

> *"I promise that I will do everything in my power to maintain the present level of spending for every welfare program now in existence. Now I realize that all of these programs are fraught with fraud. I realize that there are many beneficiaries of these programs that should not be benefiting from them. I realize that there is little realistic chance that these programs will accomplish what their*

advocates claim. I realize that we must continue to tax low and middle-income families at a rate that they cannot afford in order to continue these programs. I know that these programs are fundamentally wrong, unjust and immoral. With your support, I will keep our country on its present course of injustice."

How would potential voters react to such a statement? Is that the desire of the American People? Would our imaginary candidate get elected? Of course not. Yet that is the nature of our altruist based government. It is wrong. It is unjust. It is immoral.

There is no moral justification for John's mandate: "He that hath two coats, let him impart to him that hath none". There is no moral justification for Acts II, 44 and 45: "And all that believed were together, and had all things common; And sold their possessions and goods, and parted them to all men, as every man had need." There is no moral justification for Marx's imperative: "From each according to his ability, to each according to his needs!" There is no moral justification for the modern altruist's demand that the producers sacrifice themselves to the needy. There is no moral justification for our elected leaders to perpetuate this injustice.

Altruism and its ultimate triumph, the welfare state, tell us that need is a man's claim to reward. They tell us that the product of one man's ability and energy is rightfully consumed by those who lack ability or energy. They tell us that those who are willing to get out of bed every day and expend their lives to obtain subsistence should give that subsistence to those who are unwilling to do so. When we accept the premise that even a small part of our life is the rightful property of our needy neighbor, we accept the premise that we are rightfully his slaves. Such is the essence of altruism.

We believe that we have adequately demonstrated the chaos that is inherent in the three pillars of Christian philosophy: non-judgment, forgiveness and altruism. The reader might not agree. If that is the case, we suggest that he put these principles into practice within his family. Starting with his children he should not make any judgments about any aspect of their behavior. If he does judge a child's behavior, he should forgive any and all actions that he viewed in a negative way. And finally he should instruct his child in the morality of altruism. His child must learn that if a neighbor child needs part of his food, some of his clothing and toys of equal quantity and quality, then the neighbor child has a moral claim to those things.

PART VII

The Law and Happiness

BRUISER

Most of us have experienced something like the following. Your sister, Jane, has just called to inform you that she and her husband, Bruiser, are coming over to watch the football game with you and your family. Jane is pretty much all right. Bruiser is probably all right too. He's a good husband, and his intentions are good. It's just that his insistence on raising Little Bruiser by the "you must not damage his ego book" has produced a monster. Little Bruiser is nothing short of hell on wheels. He is the most poorly behaved brat that you've ever had the misfortune of knowing. His ego is definitely not a problem, but Jane's sanity could be in question.

There aren't enough negatives to describe that boy. He's noisy, rude, selfish, destructive, defiant, self-centered, inconsiderate, aggressive, and over-active. Simply stated, he's just totally insensitive to anyone and everyone. But he does know his limits. He knows how long his rope is with Jane, and he knows how long it is with Bruiser. Unfortunately it's much too long to suit you and your family. You heave a group sigh of relief the instant the door closes behind him as Jane and Bruiser head for home after the game.

Now try to imagine a little bruiser who has no limits: a little bruiser who has never heard the word "no". He has never been given direction of any kind to do something or not to do something. He isn't just poorly disciplined; he doesn't have a clue of the concept. He goes anywhere and does anything that he pleases at any time that the whim strikes him. He says anything that he chooses to say and in any way and at any volume he chooses, whenever and wherever he chooses to do so. He hits, scratches, bites, kicks and tears at anybody or any thing that gets in his way or that he perceives as a threat to him or to what he wants. He's blindly destructive and screams violently whenever he is challenged. Personal hygiene is nonexistent. What would you call this version of Little Bruiser, a wild animal?

You would, and you would be absolutely correct. This is the thing which we call "Man". This is man as nature made him. This is man sans village, sans rules, sans nation, sans civilization. His only relationships are to his immediate family and his small pack, and even those are ruled by force: wild, unrestrained, brute force. He is a brute. Like it or not, you and I are descendents of this man. Dear Reader, you and I are this wild thing if we have no rules. We are this wild creature, but we have been trained to operate within the rules of our particular society.

The first bruiser, i.e. man, had two fundamental needs, survival and reproduction. There were no rules to guide him in his quest for these essentials. He had his physical strength, which was puny by comparison to most of his animal cousins, and he had a brain, which unlike his animal cousins, was capable of reasoning. He didn't reason about what was right and wrong. He reasoned about how to survive which required virtually all of his time and energy. Food and shelter were as essential then as they are today, but they were more difficult to come by. Clothing wasn't even a concept. Obtaining adequate food was by itself a constant challenge. In the absence of tools, his only recourse was to scavenger for whatever he could find. We must suppose that his diet was similar to his animal predecessor, but whatever it consisted of, it was limited to those things he could find and simply pick up with his hands. Obviously, his limited choices also limited the supply.

He somehow survived and was able to reproduce. Reproduction put more pressure on the supply of food. More and more bruisers created fierce competition for the limited food supply. We can't imagine what that was like, but we can assume that it was brutal. We must assume that the weaker bruisers either perished from hunger or were driven away from the stronger bruisers to forage for food in some other territory. This would seem to be the pattern up to the point in time when bruisers learned to work together to acquire more abundant food which was made possible by taking larger prey, by cultivation and by some type of food storage. Up to this point there was only one rule, survival of the fittest. That meant survival of the strongest and the smartest.

Either voluntarily or by force the bruisers began working together in order to satisfy their common need for survival. Working together was of necessity directed by some kind of leader. At some point these primitive group leaders recognized the value of group size and made some kind of effort, either by force or by cunning, to keep dissenting members within the group. This change in behavior created the need for some kind of rules to govern their actions. It is most likely that the rules were dictates from the leader, i.e., the strongest. The rules no doubt varied by ruler, but there is no reason to doubt that in the earliest stages of this era, that the rules were tilted to favor the needs of the individual ruler. Any consideration at all for the needs of the non-ruling members of the group were likely recognized grudgingly even by the wisest of rulers, and only then because they recognized their own dependence upon the non-ruling members to satisfy their own personal needs.

These primitive rulers were the first kings, although they didn't hold a formal title as such.. As technology evolved, the kings with the most advanced technology were able to enlarge their kingdoms and power by conquering the smaller kingdoms with force. Their kingdoms and their rules, which they now called laws, were maintained by force combined with some calculated arrangements with an agent of a god. It's reasonable to assume that the mystics and witchdoctors came on the scene to explain their seemingly malevolent world even though they had no more understanding of it than their fellows did. Sometimes these mystics were one and the same as the ruler. At other times they worked in concert with the ruler in a shared power situation. They became high priests when the rulers became kings. The idea that laws should be based upon ideas and individual rights rather than upon privilege and power is a very new invention, and was not even a consideration at this time.

Rules and laws define how relationships between members of a group are to be played out. Thou shalt, and thou shalt not, as defined by Moses or his inventor are about relationships. They are the foundation of law for a major portion of the world. Those rules that are secular in nature are generally universal and have been devised by many other cultures. Man did not need a supernatural god to define how relationships need to work. He was able to do that with his own reasoning power. We will refer to them as "The Law".

Those laws served God fearing men and nations well. They benefited man in his search for happiness as long as religion maintained its moral authority. But for many they were viewed as restrictions upon personal desires, and as religious authority declined, so did adherence to The Law. We still recognize that murder and theft are bad, but we have become very tolerant, almost forgiving, of these acts. We know that bearing false witness corrupts, but we accept it. We're not sure about adultery because we're told that everybody does it.

Moses or his inventor was a wise man. He realized that a strong nation required strong family relationships and healthy relationships between its people. The Law provided specific guidelines to accomplish those ends, and thus to keep his kingdom strong. Nothing in the basic value of healthy relationships has changed since that time. A nation still has the same fundamental requirements if it is to remain strong enough to do its job. That is to provide adequate safety for its people, security of their possessions and some form of justice for its citizens.

We as individuals still have the same basic needs as the first bruiser: survival and reproduction. Of course relationships have changed drastically since then. We now live in a world where relationships are so numerous and complicated that they defy our ability to grasp them all. We still require food and shelter, and now clothing as well, but we now acquire these things through a complicated system of exchange equally as complex as our relationships. In addition to our survival we are now concerned too with our happiness. All of these things depend upon a strong community, nation and civilization. These strong entities depend upon strong, healthy relationships between all of their members. Strong, healthy relationships require The Law, but as we have seen, The Law restricts how we live and enjoy our personal lives. The weakening of religious authority has resulted in weakening the authority of The Law. That has led to the weakening of our moral character and the strength of our communities.

The common view of The Law is that of ten mandates given to Moses by a god for the purpose of controlling his people. They are "dos" and "don'ts" which essentially restrict our activities. We don't view them as a value to us as individuals, but as "values" from religious authority. The Law then seems to have no particular personal value to us except to the extent that others follow it. It protects us from harmful behaviors from them. We're particularly concerned with the rules pertaining to killing, stealing and bearing false witness, and we support them and require that others support them fairly consistently. We don't particularly like the idea of adultery, but we have come to define it as a common human weakness. We accept it rather casually. The Law lacks our personal authority and support to the extent that we fail to support some of its rules.

This lack of personal authority leads us to tolerate some breaches of The Law from other members of the group as long as those breaches seem to have no effect upon us personally. The value of the rule has now decayed. The group has little desire and no will to enforce it. If membership in the group is of value to the individual because of the groups ability to enforce rules which benefit the individual, then as a consequence, as each rule decays and falls out of use, membership in the group has less value to the individual. The value of the group itself is in the process of decay as its ability to protect its members declines.

VALUES

Individuals and society in general have established an unwritten hierarchy of the various rules of The Law, and the lower a particular rule is in the hierarchy, the less authority it has. Don't kill is at the top, and it enjoys the personal authority of virtually all members of our group. On a scale of one to ten, it probably would rate a ten. But even from its position at the top, it is under attack by the advocates of leniency. This rule is actually the core of our value system, and it still lacks unmitigated support.

Don't steal is second in terms of support with most people holding pretty strong feelings about it. But on our scale of one to ten, it would probably only get a rating of eight or nine. It's not that a lot of people have decided that stealing is okay. We have developed a rather intricate rating of kinds of theft and of the manner in which different kinds of theft are perpetrated. Ironically that rating isn't about how much is stolen or how much harm is caused. It has more to do with whether force is employed in the process. White-collar crime, for example, can have a huge impact upon scores of victims, but the perpetrators of these crimes usually receive mild punishments. On the other hand, if a man uses a weapon to steal ten dollars from a convenience store, he could spend years in a maximum-security prison.

Don't bear false witness probably ranks near but slightly below don't steal. We give it this lower rating because it is generally viewed to include the entire realm of honesty, and within that realm we have come to accept the notion that there are a multitude of forms of dishonesty. It is quite generally accepted that within that enormous realm, that there are multitudes of ways to be dishonest that are essentially harmless to anybody. Defining right from wrong within this huge gray realm is often problematic. Some people find it difficult to find fault with any kind of falsehood if harm is not immediately evident.

The issue of adultery is now viewed as a purely personal matter by an enormous number of people. It probably ranks a four or three on our scale. Even many people who have suffered from alienation of affection and divorce as a result of an adulterous spouse view adultery and its consequences as being so common that it is not a major issue. They might suffer great personal pain and be very angry or disappointed with their spouse, but they fail to see it as a problem for anybody outside of their immediate family. It is still a personal matter to them, and as such it is not the concern of anybody else.

The four rules cited above form the core of the guiding principles of relationships for virtually all of civilized existence. They are not unique and limited to the cultures from Jewish, Islamic and Christian teachings. They are universal in societies that we consider to be civilized. We will take a limited look at each in an attempt to establish whether each is critical to a healthy and safe society and to our personal happiness

DON'T KILL

Life is not a "value". It is the core, the source, of values. All values in a civilized group stem from the concept of our right to our own life. It is not a matter of the value of ones life to the group. We do not live for the group. We live for the enjoyment of our own life. Essentially a life should not be viewed as either asset or liability to the group as long as that life does not make itself into a liability. If it happens to be an asset to the group, that asset should be viewed as a bonus to the group, but it is not the responsibility or the duty of a life to serve the needs of the group.

The group, however, does have the responsibility to protect the life of each of its members. If it fails to do so, it has no value to its members. The group must first and foremost respect and protect the right to life of each of its members. If the group fails to protect the lives of its members, it completely negates its value. Membership in the group becomes worthless.. We must respect a man's right to his life, and we must help him to protect it if we are to call ourselves civilized. This respect for life is the source for the rule, don't kill. The right to one's life is primary. The rule that protects it is fundamental. Our personal happiness requires our respect for life and our support for the rule that preserves it.

DON'T STEAL

To take the property of someone else is very close to violating their right to their own existence. Property, or wealth, is the means whereby we sustain our lives. Therefore, the thief minimizes or destroys the means for living. If we think in terms of property as being the product of part of a life spent in the acquisition of it, then the thief actually takes part of ones life. For example, we work one year in order to buy a car, and the car is stolen, the thief has stolen one year of our life.

We acquire property by literally exchanging part of our lives for it. It makes no essential difference whether that is done through physical labor, performing brain surgery or creating new devices. We exchange part of our lives through whatever service we are best able to provide in exchange for money. We exchange that money for services or products that were made possible by others that exchanged part of their lives to provide those services or products. In a free society, we actually exchange a large portion of our life's time with each other. The key here is that time and life are one and the same thing. So the thief deprives us of part of our lives. The thief actually steals and uses that portion of our lives.

We should also note that within this context there are no essential differences between robbing a convenience store at gunpoint, taking a sound system from a car, extortion, fraud or embezzlement. Nor does it matter if the thief is Robinhood. These are all forms of stealing life: life used up, and life to be sustained. So a thief, regardless of the method he uses, is a parasite who uses up part of the life of his victim.

If life is the nucleus of our system of values, it's apparent that we must look upon a person's property in precisely the same manner that we look upon his life because his property is the means whereby he is able to support his life. We must view the act of stealing, regardless of the form that it takes, as an assault upon the victim's life. We must view minor shoplifting as an assault upon the lives of the entire community because the entire community has to pay for it with a part of their lives. We must view many white-collar crimes of every variety in the same way because the entire community has to pay for it with a part of their lives. All thieves of every variety steal part of the lives of others. Some steal large portions from individual lives. Some steal small portions from many, many lives. They are all parasites who live on the blood and sweat of their victims. Every theft is an assault upon the life of one or more of us. If we support the concept of life, we must totally support the rule that permits each man to sustain his own life, don't steal.

HONESTY

Moses' law was limited to the concept of not bearing false witness, but the civilized world generally interprets it to include the entire realm of personal honesty. That is as it should be. Honesty in every possible sense of the word is at the core of our relationships with each other. It is the prerequisite of good relationships. Any relationship that lacks the total honesty of all of its parties is destined to eventually deteriorate and fail to one degree or another. Honesty begets trust. It is the glue of relationships. It is the point from which we can attempt to work out differences. Dishonesty, no matter how slight, begets distrust. It is the wedge that divides us and prevents us from taking risks and seeking common ground. Honesty is the key to unity where unity is possible. Dishonesty makes unity impossible even when it would otherwise be simple to achieve. Honesty lubricates relationships. Dishonesty rips them apart.

Honesty is pretty simple to define. It's about telling the truth and keeping our word. It pertains to all of our relationships: family relationships, neighbor relationships, personal relationships and business relationships. Dishonesty is about stretching the truth or outright lying about others or ourselves. It's about attempting to gain a personal advantage through deception whether it assassinates the character of another or inflates our own character. It's about gaining advantage by cheating. It's about gaining advantage by going back on our word. Dishonesty is very similar to stealing because when we gain any type of undue advantage we are in some sense stealing it. Any gain or reduction of loss as the result of dishonesty is tainted and a theft from one or more of our relationships. It is stealing.

Each of us can imagine many examples of obvious theft resulting from dishonesty. The act of starting and spreading gossip should be included in these examples, but it might not be quite as obvious to us as others might be. The common practice of character assassination caused by starting and spreading gossip causes an abundance of pain and hardship for thousands of its victims. The intent of such gossip is always to injure its victim. Those who initiate gossip are simply malicious, and are often acting out of envy or hate. Those who spread it are perhaps only guilty of careless chatter, but the harm they cause is exactly the same as that of the person guilty of initiating it. Gossip is of the same genre as all other varieties of dishonesty. It is a form of theft.

The group and its individual members benefit from good relationships based upon all of its members being personally accountable and honest. All of the members of the group operate safely and efficiently in that environment. The opposite is true in the absence of good relationships. The group is not efficient, and it is not as safe.

DON'T COMMIT ADULTERY

Many will argue that adultery is a personal matter and of no concern or business of the group. This is perhaps true in very limited situations. Supposing that the adulterous affair is totally concealed, it has no impact on the families involved, and that no children result from it, its only impact would be on the participants. We could argue in such a case that there is no harm to anybody, and therefore there is nothing wrong with it. But this would be a most unusual case. The participants themselves must be impacted by their illicit relationship in most situations. If they have any conscience at all, they will experience some sense of guilt and a sense of confusion. These two factors alone could change their behaviors and their lives in a negative way, and those negatives are likely to exist as long as the affair endures.

It seems that there are only three possible outcomes for an adulterous affair, and none of them are positive. One possibility is for the affair to remain concealed for the lifetime of the participants in it. That would mean that both of them would live a lifetime filled with deception. The second possibility is that one of the parties will decide to end the affair at some point in time. Both parties will experience emotional trauma very similar to that of any couple that is experiencing a breakup. The final possibility is that they will decide to get married. This requires the dissolution of at least one marriage, and that of course leads to trauma for a variety of people including the perpetrators of the adulterous affair. We see then that adultery is only a personal matter in limited situations, and even when it is, it is likely to be painful to some degree.

The outcomes are often tragic if the affair becomes known, and particularly so if it leads to divorce. The participants in the affair arguably suffer the least, but even they suffer negative consequences Some of them include guilt, anguish, confusion, dislocation, lost loyalties and economic loss. At the extreme, spouses are murdered as a way to get out of the existing marriage.

Things are much more difficult for the victim spouse. They also feel guilt at times: blaming themselves for some unidentifiable personal shortcomings that caused their spouse to go astray. They are also dislocated, confused and angry. They suffer economic loss. Their values are challenged and confused. They often become rudderless and unstable, and they also have been known to commit murder as a result. Their victims sometimes are the spouse, sometimes the lover, and sometimes both.

Children are innocent victims, and they no doubt suffer in more ways, and to a greater degree, than any of the other parties. They too suffer pain, dislocation, guilt and anger. Their values are challenged, disrupted and sometimes destroyed. Their views of integrity and reliability can suffer permanent damage. The stability of family, the safe haven they have always enjoyed, vanishes, and their personal stability often suffers as a result. One of their mentors is lost, and the other one has lost part of his/her effectiveness. As a result, they don't receive the guidance that they so desperately need. They experience economic loss that can possibly impact them for the rest of their lives. This can take the form of lost opportunities in their daily lives and possibly the loss of education opportunities in the near or distant future.

These are troubled children. Their outcomes will vary in as many ways and to as many degrees as the children are in number. Good outcomes are possible and probably more common than poor outcomes. We just don't know how many of them would have been much better had they not been victims of a broken marriage in the aftermath of an adulterous affair.

There are also many not so good and many very poor outcomes. Ask your schoolteachers and principals. Talk to your police authorities, counselors, social workers and judges. Talk to a psychiatrist. Talk to the future spouses and children of these children. You will learn that these children are more likely to drop out of school and to do poorly in reading, writing and mathematics. They are more likely to have emotional and behavior problems. They have higher crime rates, and they suffer higher rates of physical and sexual abuse.

Parents of divorced couples also suffer. They have welcomed the spouse of their child into the family, and they often bond as closely to the in-law as they do to their own child. They normally form strong bonds with any grandchildren that result from the marriage. These bonds are suddenly ripped apart as another result of the adultery. If the in-law and children relocate at a great distance, these parents might never see them again, or see them so infrequently that they are deprived of being a part of the growing-up and maturing of their grandchildren. Adultery is seldom just a personal matter.

Premarital sex is a different issue. Modern attitudes on the topic are different from those on adultery, but the group sometimes pays a heavy price for this activity. It's more appropriate that we consider it as possibly irresponsible sex. We're talking about sex that results in unplanned or unwanted pregnancies, and most commonly those involving young girls.

Until the late 50's and early 60's we didn't have a lot of teen pregnancies. At least we didn't have a lot of them that we knew about. Young girls were much more careful than the modern girl is. There was a serious social stigma associated with teen pregnancy, so girls either abstained from sex until they were married, or they took precautions to avoid pregnancy. Many who did get pregnant "went away to school for a year", or they "went to take care of their aunt" for a while. The baby was born and adopted, and the girl returned home to resume her normal youthful life.

The social stigma associated with out-of-wedlock parenting has all but vanished in the last forty years. We now have baby showers and a nice little party of well-wishing and gift giving for the little mom-to-be. We have an entire array of well wishers, social workers and psychologists who spend a great deal of time and group resources to assure her that she is all right. The consequence of being irresponsible has magically been transformed into an asset. She is now important, a grown up, and virtually everybody tells her that she's wonderful even though many don't really mean it. She thinks she's wonderful too, and some of her closest friends want to be just like her. We shouldn't be the least amazed that we have an epidemic of teen pregnancies and "fatherless" children.

Those who attempt to separate the person from the person's deeds mislead themselves and us. Yes, we're all human beings with human frailties. We're all subject to making mistakes. We all have the same basic needs. We have more similarities than differences. What does differentiate us though is our actions. Our actions are the things which require the judgment of others. The mere fact that we are members of the human family does not exempt us from the judgment of others. In fact it is precisely because we are members of the human family that our actions must be judged.

Irresponsible actions don't make us any less of a human being, but they do make of us a problem for our families and for society. Irresponsible actions are destructive to personal and group relationships. Irresponsible actions cause grief and pain to others, and that is why they must be judged. Our actions don't determine what we are, but they do determine who we are. Irresponsible actions are not all right, and the people who act irresponsibly are not all right either. Bringing babies into this world before we are psychologically and financially prepared to do so is totally irresponsible. It is not fair to the young parents who do it or to the group. It is mostly unfair to the baby.

Part of nature's scheme is to ensure the propagation of every species. Residing within the medulla oblongata, the most primitive part of the human brain, is one of the few remaining true instincts of man, the drive to reproduce. It's only goal is to ensure propagation. It is as natural as any part of man can be. Like the same drive in our animal cousins, it has the power at times to preempt even our need for personal safety. It is reasonably safe to say that nothing can cause us to become so stupid so fast as getting caught up in the scent of a sexual relationship: a new relationship in the case of a married person; any sexual relationship in the case of a young, immature person. There should be no wonder to anybody that we have such things as adultery and other forms of irresponsible sex when we realize the power of this natural instinct. We can blame our primitive instinct if we choose, but that doesn't justify irresponsible sex any more than our basic selfishness justifies any other type of social crime.

HAPPINESS AND THE RULES

Murder, theft, dishonesty and adultery have negative and frequently destructive consequences. The first three can have an impact upon a broader range of our group, but they can have a very negative impact upon those who are close to us as well. Adultery takes its greatest toll upon those who are closest to us: our spouse, our children, our own parents and usually upon ourselves. So we think that these four rules are valid. They make sense if we want to have a strong group: one that protects our individual rights and our right to life. We can see that each of them is a benefit to each of us as individuals. They are not just arbitrary mandates that were handed to us from the supernatural. They are rules that were created by the mind of man for the enrichment of man.

A question may arise as to the relative importance of each of the rules. We could certainly say that the rule about not killing is obvious, but the rule about adultery isn't so obvious. So there might be a question whether the rule about adultery is important. Perhaps the best and simplest test of any of the rules is to imagine society without it. What would life be like in a society where there was not even such a concept? It should be apparent that the disregard of the basic rules takes us right back to life in the jungle with the bruisers where there is only one rule; that of brute strength?

Virtually all actions taken by the rest of us have consequences for other people as well as for ourselves. It is those consequences to others that make the rules of society essential. If we choose not to be a hermit, it is incumbent upon us to play by the rules. If it is possible for us to question whether as individuals we might want to disregard one or more of the rules, we should ask ourselves whether we would tell our family about it, or if we would want our actions reported in the newspaper or on the six o'clock news.

The rules are not only essential for a strong, secure group, but they are also essential for our personal happiness. The appearance that they can get in the way of our happiness at times is just that, an appearance, an illusion. We can actually say that it is virtually impossible to find happiness in their absence. They provide the social mechanism and conditions necessary for our search for happiness. The rules restrain us from taking actions that are harmful to ourselves and to others, but they do not put any limits on our potential for happiness. One of the conditions for happiness is self-acceptance. Self-acceptance is only possible to those who are totally honest with themselves. The totally honest person harbors no illusion that breaking the rules will make him happy. He knows in fact that the exact opposite is true.

ABOUT THE OUTLAWS

Religion's loss of moral authority perhaps culminated in the 1960's. The loss of religious authority was inevitable because it was based upon a mythical god who gave us what seemed to be arbitrary rules. As more people began to question the existence of a god, the rules carried less and less weight in the minds of more and more people. We have now reached the logical collision of the contradictory Judeo-Christian ethos. We have minimized the importance of those principles of Moses' law that we don't see as a direct threat to our civilization and ourselves, and we herald the most dangerous principles of Christianity: non-judgment, forgiveness and altruism. Some of the noisiest people in our society are those yelling for mercy and forgiveness of every type of crime because according to them all men are inherently evil and weak. Most of us go along because we're unwilling to cast the first stone. The result is confusion and moral decay.

Man is not inherently evil and weak. Each man and each woman is an individual, and each of us *chooses* how to live our lives. Some choose to live by the rules. Some choose to ignore the rules or mistakenly believe that they are above the rules, but we must all abide by the rules if we want to continue to live in a civilized world. The rules are important and, we are *capable* of living by them. Man does not have some innate evil tendency that prevents him from doing the right thing. Man was not created evil. In fact, man was not created. He is a descendent of the natural, the wild, but that does not mean that he is incapable of making moral rules and living by them. Some of those who tell us that we are inherently evil make their livelihood from our guilt. The others use our alleged guilt to excuse the guilt of the immoral. We should not allow either of them to continue that fraud.

Violators of the rules are criminals, the enemies of civilization. Most of them probably don't see themselves in that light, because they don't understand the significance and the value of the rules to civilization and to themselves. But if we value life itself, we must value the "values" that protect it. The rules we reviewed play an important role in that regard. Deviant behavior has now become so common ("everybody does it") that some of us no longer consider it to be deviant. It is the norm in a large segment of our society. We live in a less stable and less safe world as a result.

Civilization is impossible in the absence of rules. Civilization is impossible in the absence of judgment. It's not enough that we have judges and juries to pass judgment in civil and criminal cases. All of us must pass judgment upon the events that surround our everyday lives. To the degree that we allow the rules to be compromised, we compromise our own safety and happiness. If we condone bad behavior with our silence, we encourage additional bad behavior. We must not compromise with bad behavior. We must not sanction bad behavior with our silence.

THIS IS IT

Life might seem pointless to some people if there is no eternal life. But if we need some external source to point out the point of our own lives, we're missing out on living. The point is that there is no point. That is in fact the beauty of it. That leaves it up to us to decide for ourselves what our life is about, and what it is going to be about. We're free to make it about anything that we choose. So the important questions aren't "Is this it?" or "Is that all there is?" It's adequately apparent that the answer to both questions is, "yes". The important question is "What do I want to do with it?" Consider the infinity of possibilities. Each of us is free to choose our own path, and if we want to change paths tomorrow, we can do that too. If there were a point, it would be to love every moment of life right up to the last one. If you need something to believe in, believe in yourself and your right to enjoy your life and the fruit of your own labor.

> "Ah, make the most of what we yet may spend,
>   Before we too into the Dust descend;
>   Dust into Dust, and under Dust, to lie,
>   Sans Wine, sans Song, sans Singer, and___sans End!" (3)

Epilogue

"and let them have dominion over the fish of the sea, and over the fowl of the air, and over the cattle, and over all the earth," Genesis: 1, 26

Man has had a long journey from his beginnings as a wandering scavenger to his present state of master of his fate. It's noteworthy that the purveyors of superstition exerted considerable energy and spilled rivers of blood to discourage his dominion over all the earth. They discouraged education of the masses, suppressed scientific thought, asserted that man's ability to reason was flawed and routinely tortured and murdered dissenters. Those activities were not simply about who had the right answers about and access to the right god. They were about the highest stakes in the history of mankind. They were about the battle for man's mind. That battle began when the first witchdoctor recognized the power he possessed as long as his tribesmen believed in his magic. He was the first version of the thought police. The battle is still being waged and for the same reason, thought control. Thought control is the ultimate power.

There should be no doubt that the world would be a totally different place if the purveyors of superstition had won the battle for man's mind. The earth would still be flat, and the fastest ships would be powered by slaves. But mans trust in his own mind, and his determination to know the truth about his existence, have brought him to his present state. There is every reason to believe that he is at the threshold of even more exciting and rewarding times. While we eagerly anticipate our future, let's take a moment to reflect upon the true nature of man: the nature that was necessary to bring him to where he is today.

Man is the thinker; the only rational animal on our planet. Man is the questioner, the challenger and the seeker of truth. He asks why things are as they are, what if they were different and how they could be better. Man is the tinkerer, the experimenter and the inventor. Man is the planner, the organizer and the builder. Man is the teacher. Man is the poet, the teller of stories and the singer of songs. Man is the jester. Man is the athlete. Man is the helper and the physician. Man is the maker of good soup and fine wine. Man is the creator of the rule of ideas in place of the rule of force.

Man is genetically restless and selfish, but a rational man is capable of, and does channel his restless, selfish nature into activities that are heroic. He has the potential to accomplish a galaxy of wonderful and beautiful things. Rational man is good. He acts for his own benefit, and when he is at his best, when his thoughts go beyond the known, when he dares to risk everything for his dream, he might build a better mousetrap. If he does, he benefits, and his actions provide a benefit to all around him.

Many thousands of men and women have made major contributions toward the improvement of our way of living. We indeed owe them a debt that can never be repaid. As we look back on mans progress, we might be tempted to think that if one man had not created something that another would have. That is a dangerous and unfounded assumption. If that one man had not done it, it might never have been done, and everything that followed from it could never have happened. The chance that it might never have been done is equally as good as the chance that it would have been done. Let's think for a moment about a few primitive heroes and what our existence might be like had they not thought about something and attempted it.

What if it had never occurred to somebody to mount a horse? Would we still be afoot? How much courage did it take to do what had never been thought of before and to do it without the benefit of a bridle and saddle? What if nobody had thought about milking a cow or a goat, and nobody ever tried to plant seeds Would we still be scavengers? What if nobody ever thought about building a shelter? What if nobody ever thought about using an animal skin for clothing? What if nobody had thought about harnessing fire or of storing water? There are only two possible answers to these what ifs. Man would still be a scavenger or he would be extinct.

Those prehistoric adventurers and experimenters made all later innovations possible. Man harnessed water and electricity. He developed mass production. He invented the printing press. He put hot and cold running water in his home. He invented toilet tissue and sewer systems. He invented plastic and the memory chip. His creative activity seems to expand geometrically with each new invention. He continues to invent creature comforts and efficiencies at an incredible pace. Most of us take for granted literally thousands of machines, gadgets and conveniences in our homes, in our cars and at our place of employment. We are more productive, we are more comfortable and we have more time for leisure activities than we could have dreamed to be possible just a few generations ago.

Most of us are the benefactors of our wonderful lifestyle without directly contributing to it. We operate the machines and the gadgets that make us more efficient, but we had absolutely nothing to do with their creation. We are the benefactors of the minds and of the risk taking of the creators whether it was that first man to mount a horse or the inventor of toilet tissue.

We must keep in mind that all new mental concepts, the core ideas that lead to innovation, are the product of individual minds. There is no such thing as a group mind. Only individual men and women can have a new idea, a new concept, or a new vision. Others might assist in the development or the refinement of something, but an idea can only occur in an individual mind. It is ideas, the product of individual minds, that have made our present lifestyle possible. The ideas of individuals are what will make improvements on that lifestyle possible.

The creators do what they do for their personal benefit. This was true of the first man to mount a horse, and it is true of the modern entrepreneur. We don't know the motivation for that first horseback ride, but we must assume that the potential rider envisioned some personal benefit. We know that the motivation for the entrepreneur is to make money. Personal gain is the motivation in each instance. They experience personal gain if they are successful. They experience personal loss if they fail. The rest of us don't even know about the experiment if they fail, but if they succeed, we enjoy an improvement in our personal lifestyle. The entrepreneur cannot cause loss for us, but he can cause improvement for us.

We give him money for his product if he creates something that we like. If he creates something that a lot of us like, a lot of us give him money. He becomes wealthy. We must be clear that *we* did not make him wealthy. *His idea and his work* made him wealthy. We voluntarily exchanged some of our money in exchange for the use of his idea and work.

The modern altruist tells us that because society made the entrepreneur wealthy he has a moral duty to *give back* to society. That is inverted logic. He didn't take anything from society in the first place. Society, assuming that it knows what it wants, is already happier with its situation than it was before he created what it likes so much. He gave society something that it wanted. Society rewarded him with what he wanted. Both sides are satisfied with the exchange. There is no debt. What the entrepreneur can't do is be rewarded by future generations that will also benefit from his creation; just as the first man to mount a horse can't be rewarded for his contribution to this generation. We non-creators, without personal effort or risk, are the benefactors of the entrepreneurs. The ideas and work of the experimenters and creators have virtually freed man from the whims of nature. They owe us no more.

The ideas and bravery of some men have freed many of us from the rule of the sword and the kings. The American Revolution was the high point of that political revolution. It paved the way and created the model for political freedom. Usually overlooked, but equally important, it paved the way for freedom from the priest. The formal separation of church and state did much more than to outlaw a government religion. It made it possible to reject the concept of any supernatural being without the risk of political and physical persecution. Millions have freed themselves from the priest as a side benefit of the American Revolution.

The intent of this book is to encourage and assist the reader to escape from the superstition that makes the priest possible. Once that is accomplished, one can intellectually challenge the anti-man foundation of Christian philosophy: non-judgment, forgiveness and self-sacrifice. When one realizes that there is no moral/ethical authority for self-sacrifice, i.e., altruism, one can philosophically challenge the existence of any form of a welfare state. It should be apparent that self-sacrifice and personal freedom are mutually exclusive.

Hopefully, Dear Reader, this book has helped to free you from the philosophy and the power of the priest. At the same time, we must realize that there are certain rules that we must observe if we are to be happy and safe. Some of the commandments, those that deal with our relationships with one another, form a good foundation for those rules. When we realize that sound relationships are essential to our happiness, and that those rules are about our relationships with each other and with ourselves, we can embrace them, and we can ask that all men should do the same. Admittedly they might be no more than hand-me-down conventions of our society, but unless we can find better rules, we must live by them. The future of civil man depends upon it.

Bibliography

Foreword

1. Jefferson, Thomas, *Thomas Jefferson Writings*, p. 902, Literary Classics of the United States, Inc., New York, Fifth Printing

2. Rand, Ayn, *The Virtue of Selfishness*, p. 93, New York, Signet, 1964

Part I

1. Hamilton, Edith, *Mythology*, p. 14, Boston, Mentor Books, Little, Brown and Company 1963

2. Williams, Henry Smith, *The Historians' History of the World*, volume XXIII, p. 262, USA, The Encyclopaedia Britannica, Inc., 1926

3. Ibid., p. 31

4. Ibid., p. 161

5. Durant, Will, *The Story of Civilization, Part VI, The Reformation*, p. 438, New York, Simon and Schuster, 1957

6. Merton, Thomas, *Zen and the Birds of Appetite*, p. 125, copyright 1968 by The Abbey of Gethsemani, Inc., New Directions Publishing Corp.

7. Durant, Will, *The Story of Civilization, Part VI, The Reformation*, p. 366, New York, Simon and Schuster, 1957

8. Ibid., p. 386

9. Ibid., p. 386

Part II

1. Rand, Ian, *The Voice of Reason*, p. 70, New York, Penguin Books, 1990

2. Durant, Will, *The Story of Civilization, Part VI, The Reformation*, p. 370, New York, Simon and Schuster, 1957

3. Ibid., p. 359

4. Jefferson, Thomas, Letter to Francis Hopkinson, March 13, 1789, *Thomas Jefferson Writings*, p. 941, New York, Library Classics of the United States, 1984

Part III

1. Durant, Will, *The Story of Civilization, Part VI, The Reformation*, p. 354, New York, Simon and Schuster, 1957

Part IV

1. Ibid, p. 341

Part V

1. Kamenka, Eugene, *The Portable Karl Marx*, p. 541, New York, Penguin Books, 1983

Part VII

1. *Rubaiyat of Omar Khayyam*, verse XXIV

0-595-22048-7